Letts

gets you through

PHONICS
SUCCESS
WORKBOOK

Ages 5–6

PHONICS

WORKBOOK

LOUIS FIDGE AND
CHRISTINE MOORCROFT

Contents

Contents

Alternative spellings for vowel phonemes

Alternative spellings for consonant phonemes

Alternative consonant pronunciations

What have I learned?

Introduction

Phonics for children (ages 5 to 6)

Phonics is the relationship between sounds (phonemes) and letters or groups of letters (graphemes). Learning phonics involves listening to sounds, recognising sounds and discriminating between sounds as well as learning how sounds are represented by letters.

In addition to learning phonics, children should have opportunities to:
- read and enjoy stories, poems, rhymes and jingles
- read non-fiction texts, including signs, labels, captions and notes.

How this book is organised

Letters of the alphabet (p. 6–11) further develops understanding of upper- and lower-case letters, and alphabetical order.

Vowel digraphs introduces vowel sounds spelled with two letters: ay, ou, oy, ir, ea, aw, ew, oe, au, ie, ey for the 'ay' sound, and ey for the 'ee' sound.

Split digraphs features words with long vowel sounds (such as the 'i' in 'kite') that are spelled with two letters separated by a consonant (e.g. i–e in 'kite', a–e in 'bake').

Alternative vowel pronunciations introduces different ways of pronouncing vowels that have already been introduced. For example, the letter 'i' has been introduced for the 'i' sound in 'tip', 'bit' and so on, but it can also be pronounced in the same way as 'igh' in 'high' in words such as 'tiny', 'iPad', 'mild'.

Alternative spellings for vowel sounds introduces different ways of spelling vowel sounds such as the 'or' sound in 'for'. This sound can also be spelled 'ore', 'oor' or 'our'.

Alternative spellings for consonant phonemes introduces different and more unusual ways of spelling the consonant sounds 'w' (wh), 'f' (ph), 'ch' (tch and tu) and 'j' (dge).

Alternative consonant pronunciations introduces less common ways of pronouncing consonants 'ch' (as 'k' in 'Christmas' and as 'sh' in 'chef'). Other unusual consonants introduced are 'ci' and 'ti' for 'sh' (as in 'special' and 'mention'), 's' for 'z' (as in 'please'), other 'c' and 'g' sounds and the 'zh' sound represented by 's' in words such as 'treasure'.

Silent letters features 'g', 'k', 'w', 'b' and 't' in words such as 'gnaw', 'knee', 'dumb' and 'listen'.

What have I learned?

This section provides activities to help you and your child assess what has been learned. There are no pictures to use as clues – your child will use phonics knowledge only to read the words.

What the words mean

blend	Where two or more letters are sounded individually and then blended to read or spell a word.
consonant	The letters of the alphabet that are not **vowels**. Y can be used as either a vowel or a consonant. In English, **consonant phonemes** can be represented by more than one letter, for example: ch, th, sh, ng.
digraph	The two letters representing a single phoneme (sound), e.g. 'ay' in 'play'.
grapheme	The letter(s) that represent a **phoneme**. For example, the following graphemes can all represent the same phoneme: i (ibex, silent), y (cry, deny), igh (high, night), ie (cries, tried), i–e (bite, rice).
phoneme	The smallest unit of sound in a word, for example: 'cat' has three phonemes, represented by the letters c, a and t. A phoneme can be represented by two or more letters: f**or**t, h**igh**, n**eigh**.
split digraph	The two letters representing a single sound that are separated by another letter, e.g. the a–e in 'make'.
vowel	The letters a, e, i, o and u. Y can also be used as a vowel, e.g. gym, rely. In English, some vowel **phonemes** are represented by groups of letters: or, ar, oo, igh, eigh.

Regional pronunciation will affect how your child pronounces some words. For example, the 'u' sound (as in 'cup', 'but' and 'sun') is often pronounced differently in different regions. This regional difference is not wrong.

ACKNOWLEDGEMENTS

The author and publisher are grateful to the copyright holders for permission to use quoted materials and images.

Cover, P01 ©Igorrita/Shutterstock.com; P30 ©iStockphoto/Thinkstock; P33 ©iStockphoto/Thinkstock; P37 ©iStockphoto/Thinkstock; P43 ©iStockphoto/Thinkstock; P46 ©iStockphoto/Thinkstock; P47 Andy Roberts/2idesign, P46 ©iStockphoto/Thinkstock; P51 © Robert Harness / iStockphoto.com; P57 ©iStockphoto/Thinkstock

All other images are ©Jupiterimages or Letts Educational, an imprint of HarperCollins Publishers Ltd.

Every effort has been made to trace copyright holders and obtain their permission for the use of copyright material. The author and publisher will gladly receive information enabling them to rectify any error or omission in subsequent editions. All facts are correct at time of going to press.

Published by Letts Educational
An imprint of HarperCollins Publishers Ltd
1 London Bridge Street
London SE1 9GF

ISBN 9780008294236
First published 2013
This edition published 2018

10 9 8 7 6 5 4 3

Design and Illustration © Letts Educational, an imprint of HarperCollins Publishers Limited

Text © Louis Fidge and HarperCollins Publishers Ltd

All rights reserved. No part of this publication may be reproduced, stored in a retrieval system, or transmitted, in any form or by any means, electronic, mechanical, photocopying, recording or otherwise, without the prior permission of Letts Educational.

British Library Cataloguing in Publication Data.

A CIP record of this book is available from the British Library.

Commissioning editor: Tammy Poggo
Authors: Louis Fidge and Christine Moorcroft
Project editor: Charlotte Christensen
Cover design: Paul Oates
Inside concept design: Letts Educational
Text design and layout: Planman Technologies
Artwork: Nigel Kitching, Geoff Ward and Planman Technologies
Production: Natalia Rebow
Printed and bound in Great Britain by Martins the Printers

Animal alphabet

Letters a–m

Say the name of each animal.

Write the letters for the first sound.

Write the first letter in the box.

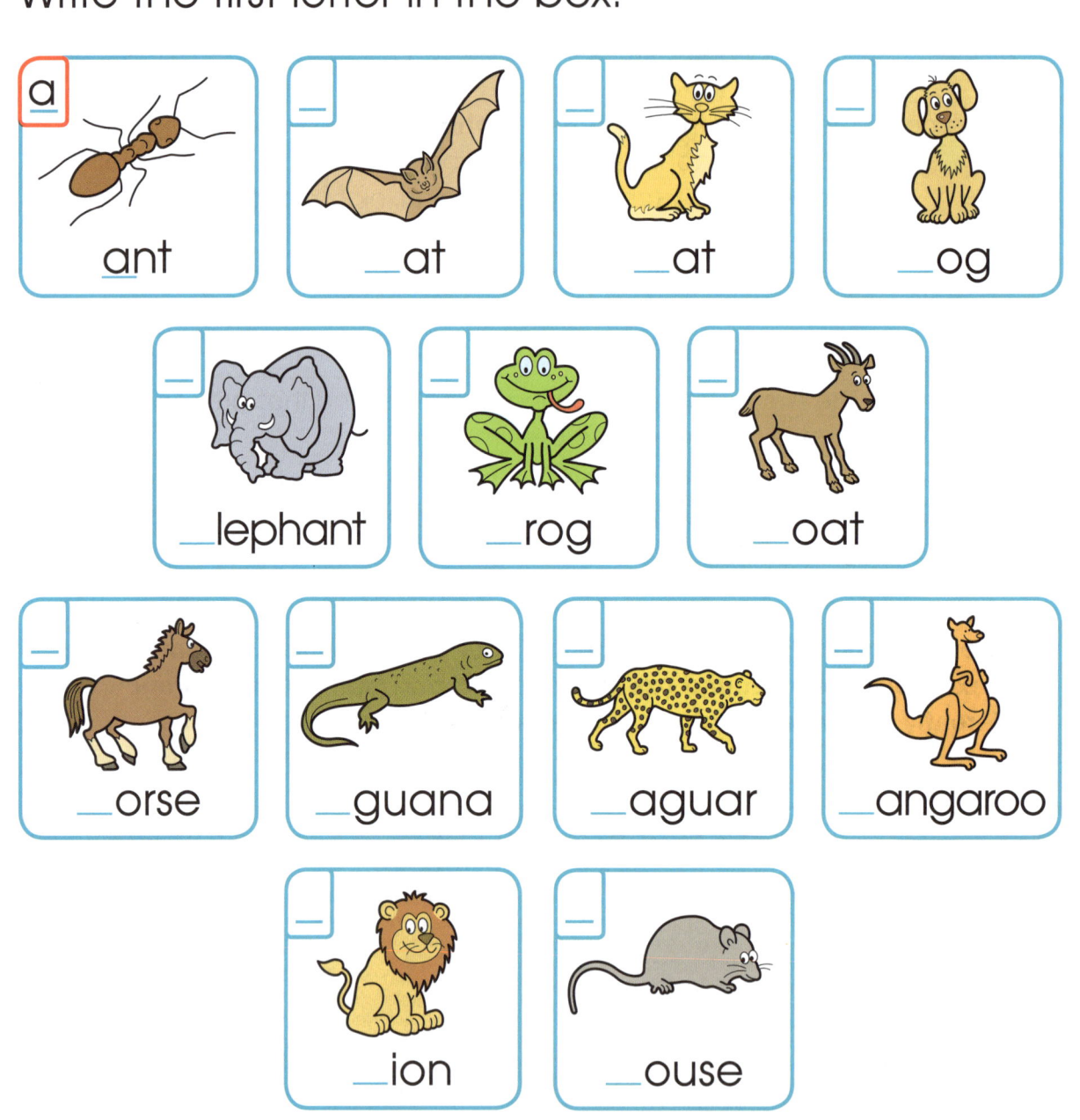

a   ant

___at

___at

___og

___lephant

___rog

___oat

___orse

___guana

___aguar

___angaroo

___ion

___ouse

Parent's tip   Ask your child to name the animal in each picture. Give help where necessary (especially for the more unusual animals, such as iguana). Then ask him/her to name the animal in the first picture. Ask your child to say the sound the word begins with and then to name the letter and write it in the box.

Letters n–z

Say the name of each animal.
Write the letters for the first sound.
Write the first letter in the box.

n | <u>n</u>ewt

__strich

__anda

___ail

__abbit

__nake

__ortoise

__mbrella bird

__ulture

__olf

__-ray fish

__ak

__ebra

Alphabetical order

Rocket alphabet

Take the rocket to each star in order.

Dot-to-dot alphabet

Join up the dots in alphabetical order to make a picture.

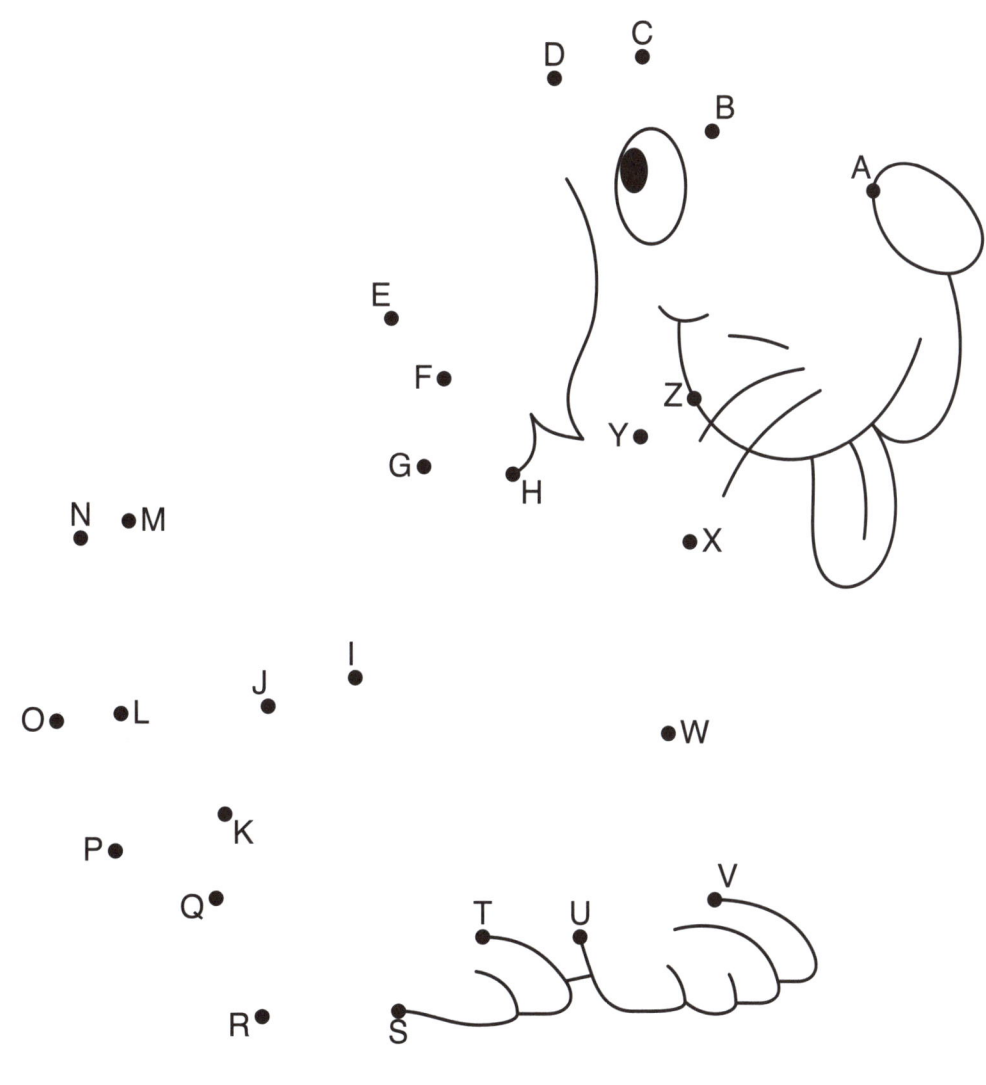

Parent's tip

Ask your child to find the first letter of the alphabet and say its name. Ask 'What comes next?' Ask questions such as: 'Which letter comes after h?', 'What comes after t?' and so on. After your child has completed the page ask: 'Which letter comes before b?', 'What comes before h?' and so on.

Upper- and lower-case letters

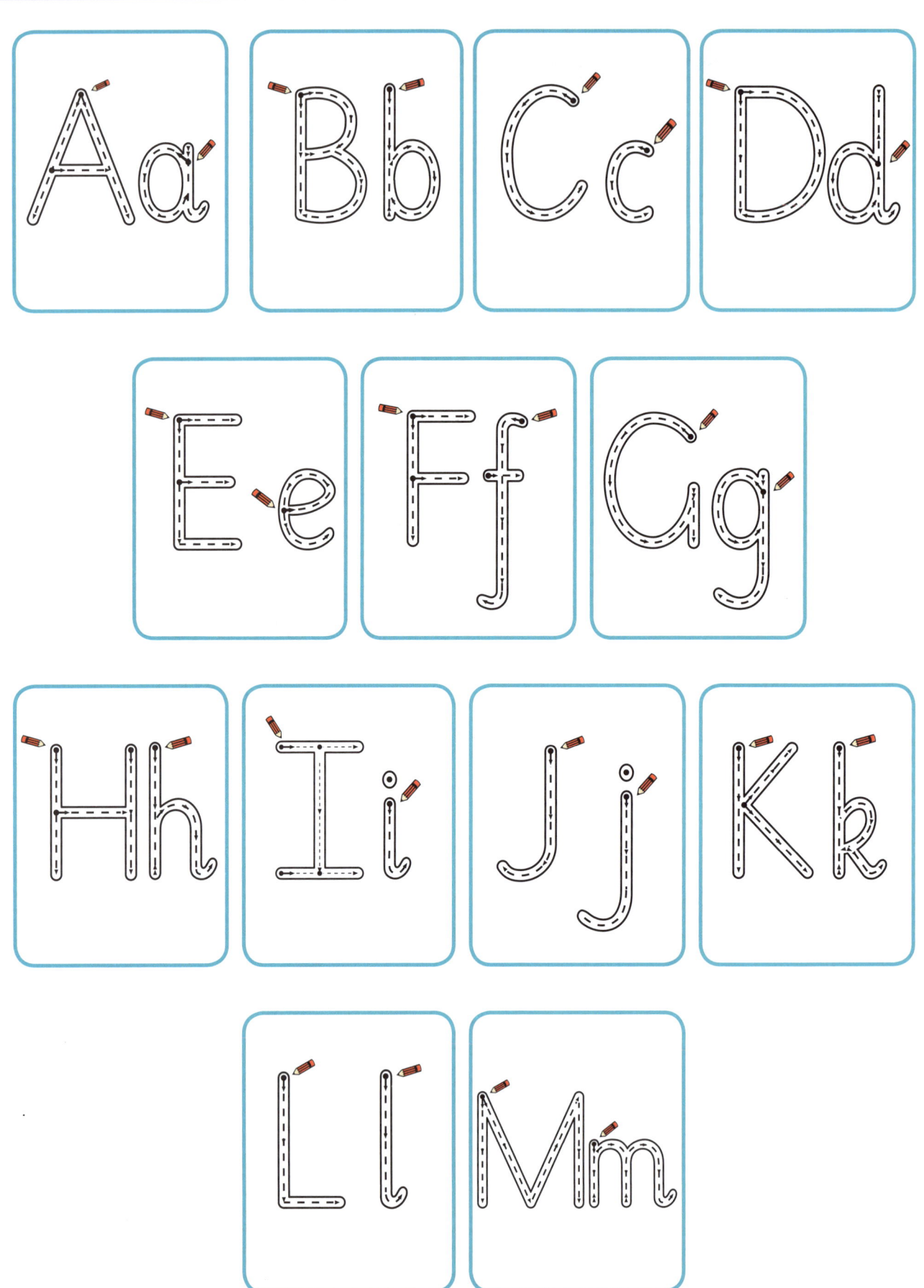

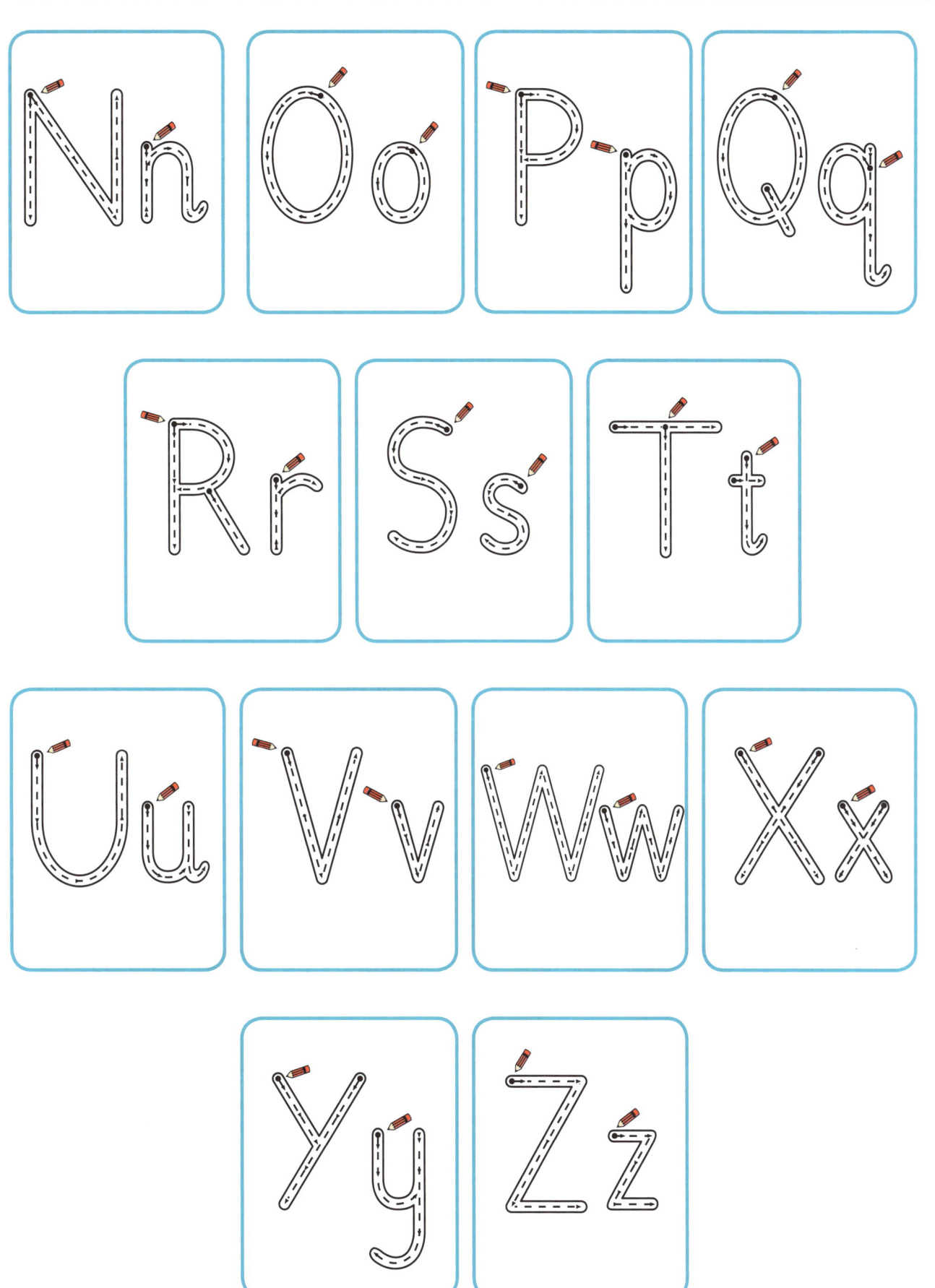

Words with ay

Read the rhyme

Circle **ay** in the rhyme.

I say, I say! Let's play today.

Hop away! Skip away!

May I play today?

Make the words

Make some words. Write the words. Read the words.

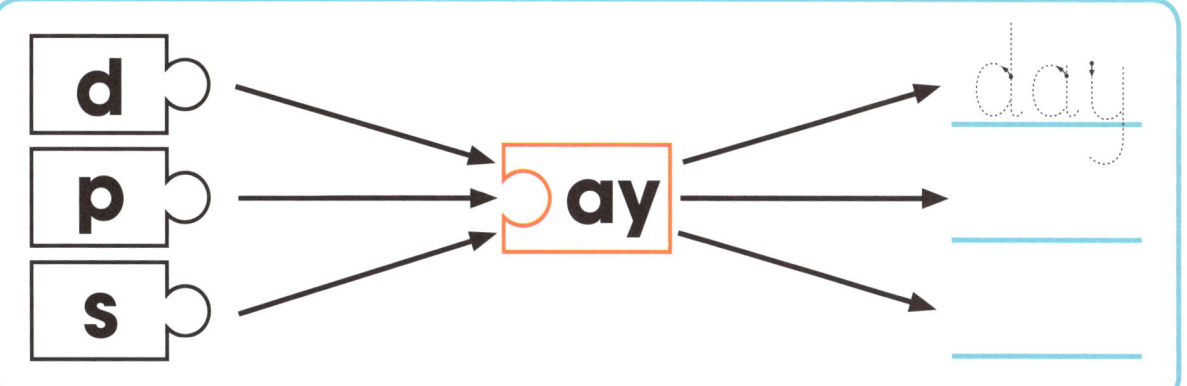

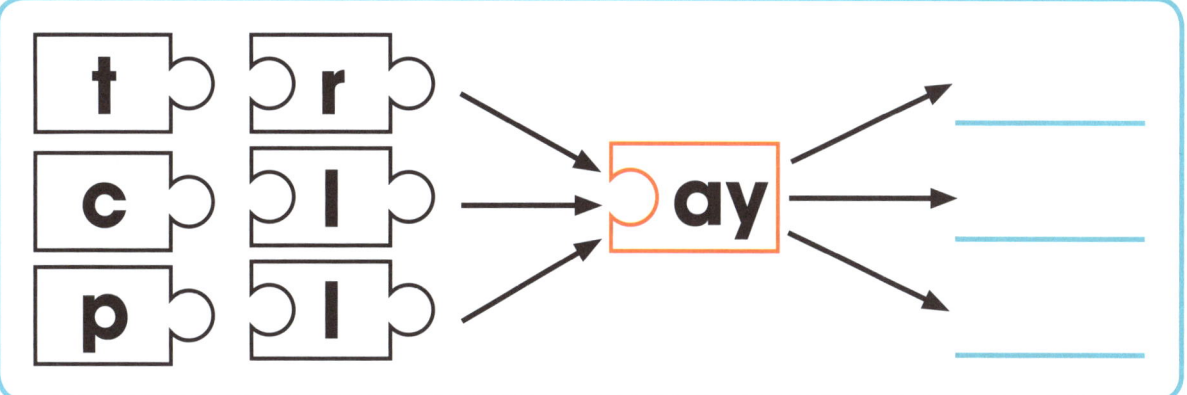

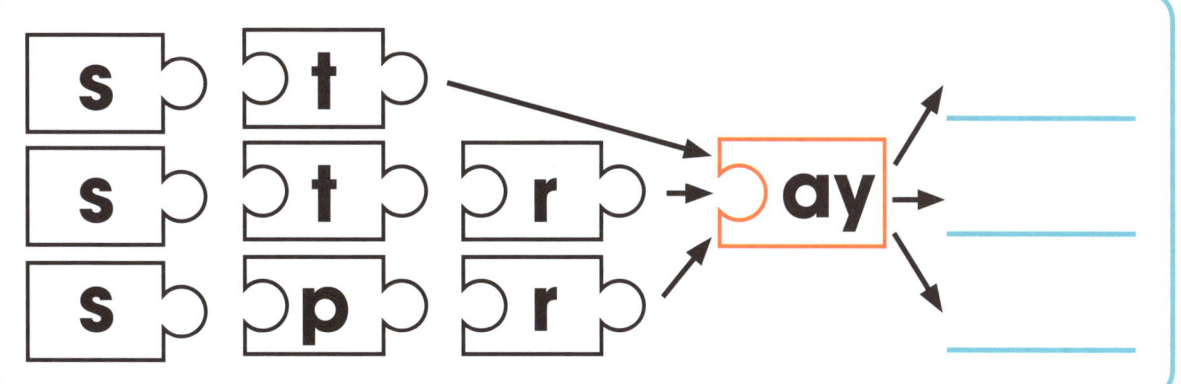

Parent's tip

Before beginning this page you could encourage your child to have fun making up rhymes. For example: 'Go away to Bombay', 'Don't play on the motorway', 'Stay on the pathway', 'I'll play with the spray', 'May has a tray of clay', 'Play with Jay', 'There's some hay in the bay'.

Words with ou

Read the rhyme

Circle **ou** in the rhyme.

The roundabout goes round and round.

We bound around for a pound.

We shout and shout.

On the roundabout.

Words with ou

Match the words

Read the words.
Match pairs of rhyming words.

Write the words.
Colour **ou** in the words.

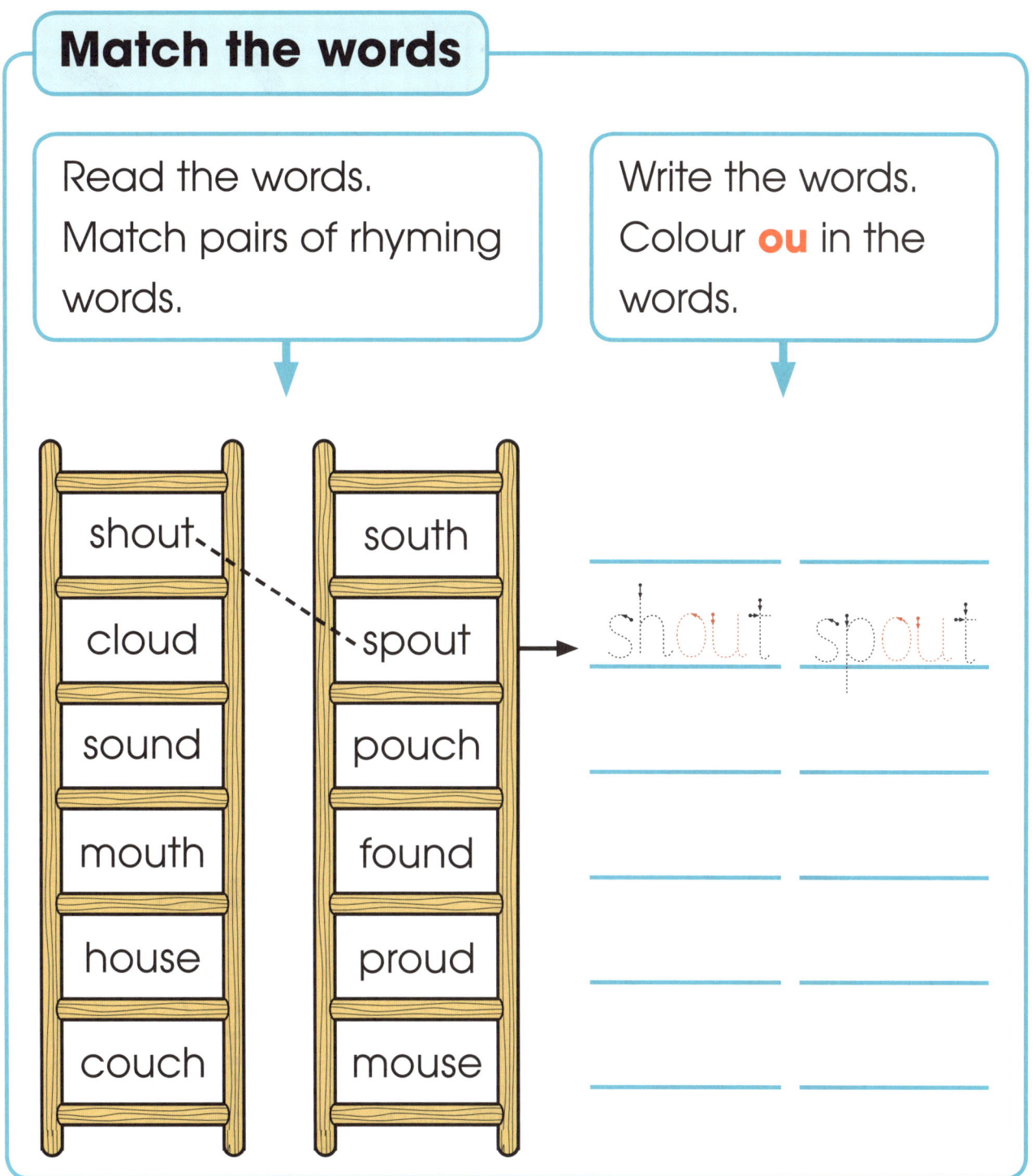

shout	south
cloud	spout
sound	pouch
mouth	found
house	proud
couch	mouse

shout   spout

Words with oy

b | oy

boy

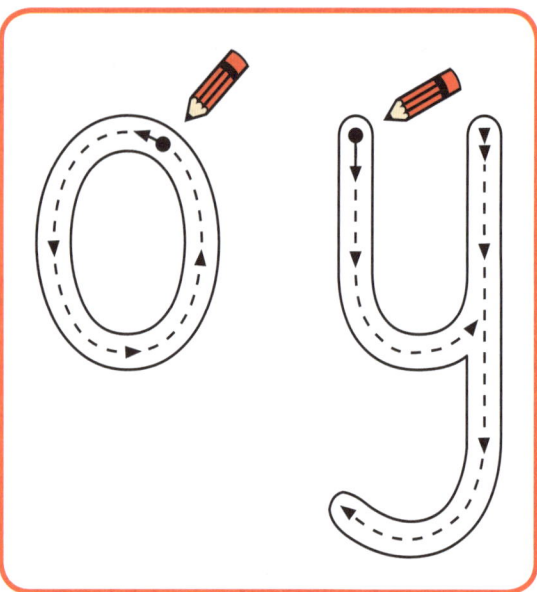

Read the rhyme

Circle **oy** in the rhyme.

Joy is a girl. Roy is a boy.

They fell out over a toy.

"Let's enjoy it, not destroy it,

Don't annoy me," said Joy to Roy.

Words with oy

Make the words

Make some words. Read the words.

oy   b___   t___   enj___   ann___

oy   empl___   cowb___   destr___

Write the words

Write the words in the grid.
Put one sound in each box.

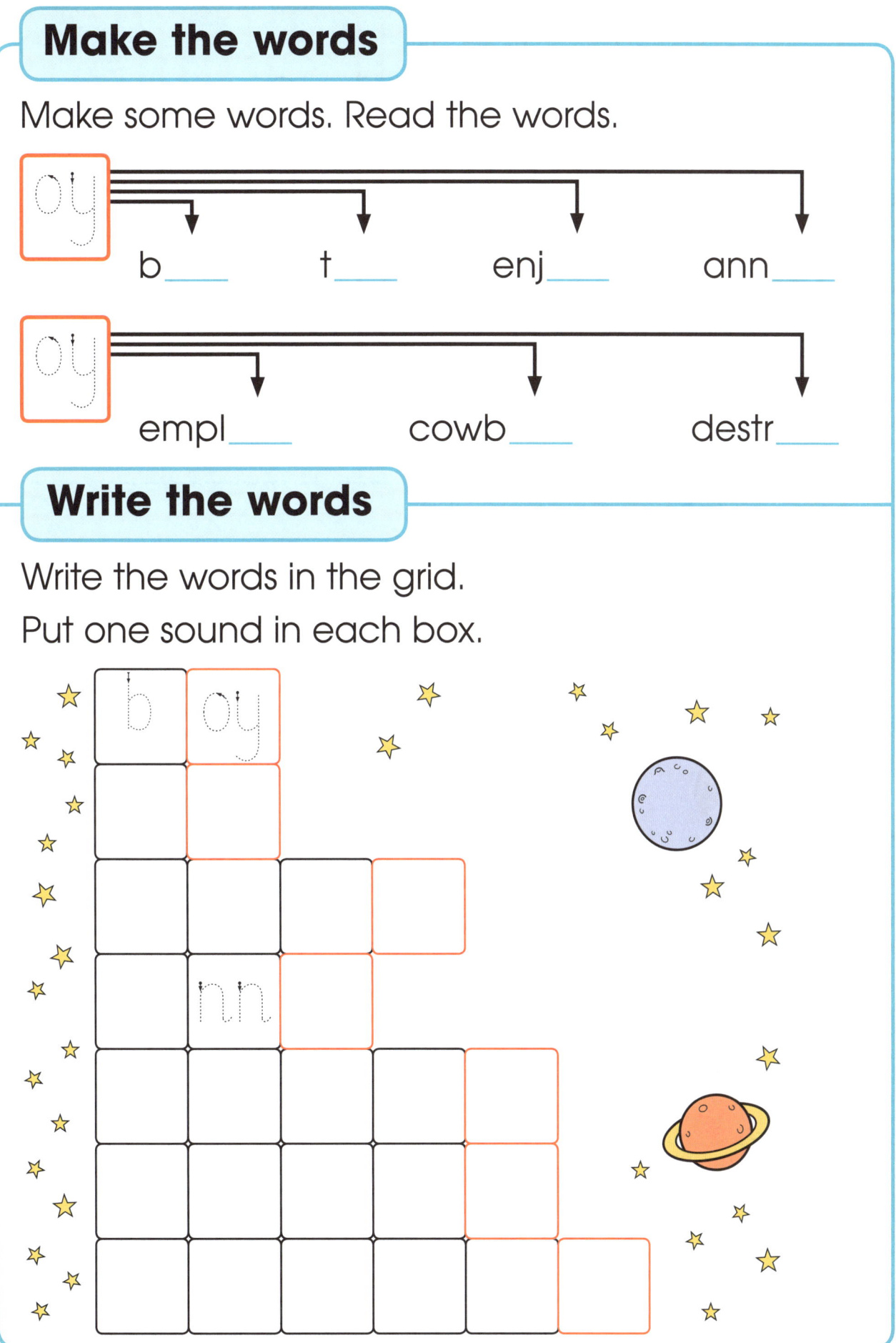

Words with ir

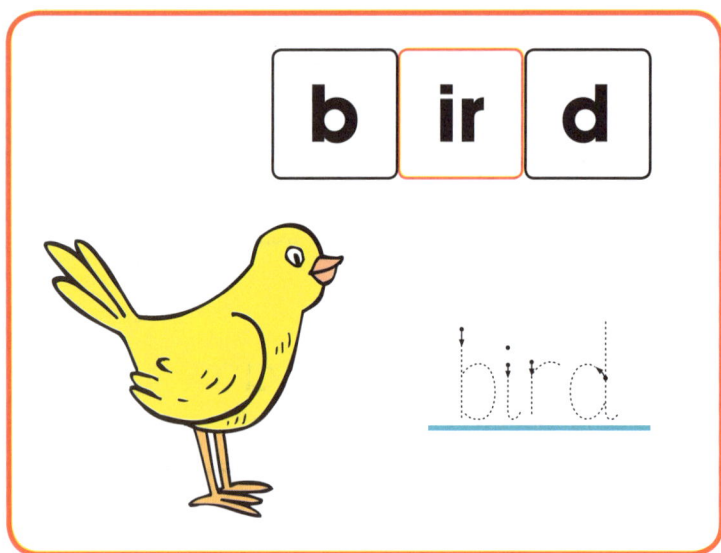

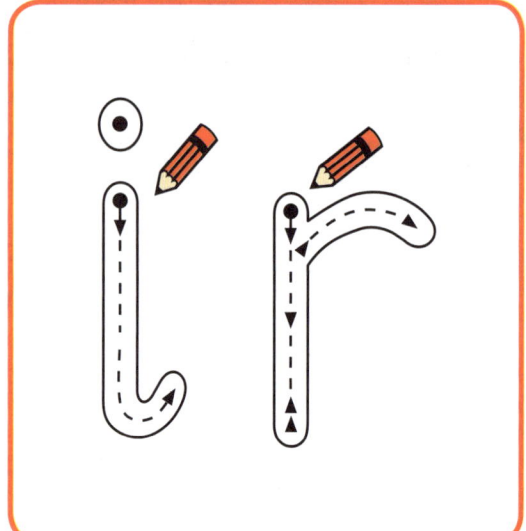

Read the rhyme

Circle **ir** in the rhyme.

The first girl is thirsty.

The second girl's skirt is dirty.

The third girl, I'm glad to say, is happy on her birthday!

Match the words

Read the words.
Match pairs of rhyming words.

Write the words.
Colour **ir** in the words.

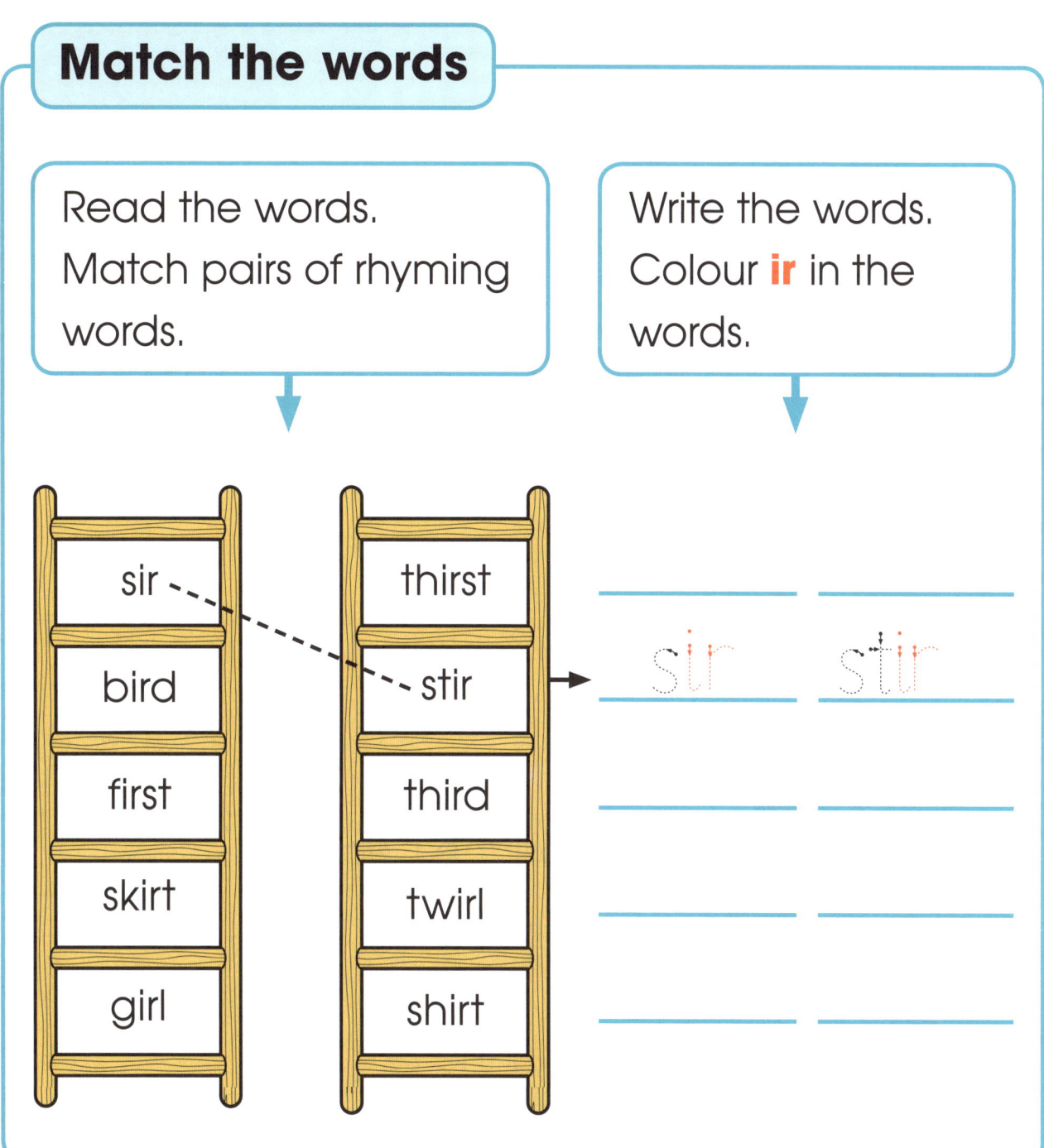

sir

bird

first

skirt

girl

thirst

stir

third

twirl

shirt

sir   stir

Parent's tip

If necessary, explain that there are different ways of spelling the same sound. Write 'ir' and ask your child to say the sound 'ir' and give some examples of words he/she has learned that have 'ir' in them. Read 'sir' and 'stir' aloud (emphasising the 'ir' sounds). Ask your child what they notice about the sounds at the ends of the words. Point out the line that joins them 'because they rhyme'. Say the next word in the left-hand ladder ('bird'), emphasising 'ird'. Tell your child that there is a rhyming word in the other ladder. Read the words in the right-hand ladder. Ask which word rhymes with 'bird'.

Words with ea

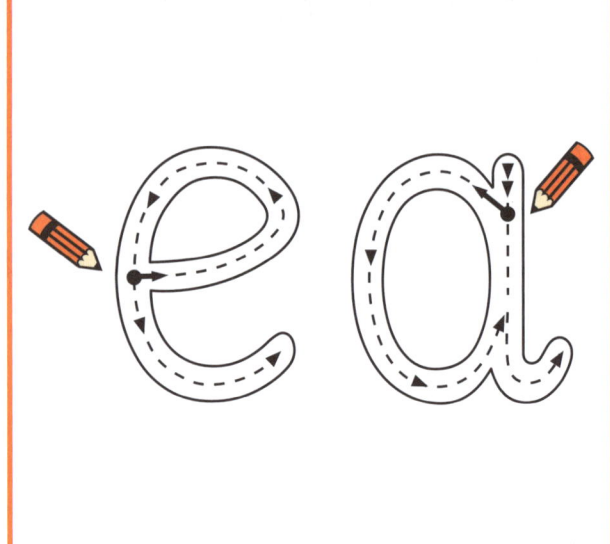

Read the rhyme

Circle **ea** in the rhyme.

Play on the beach.

Swim in the sea.

Sit on a seat.

Eat your tea!

Read the words

Read the words. Write the words.

| ea → t | s → ea → l | r → ea → d |
| eat | | |

| t → ea → ch | l → ea → p | b → ea → k |
| | | |

Write the words

Write the correct word under each picture.

Words with aw

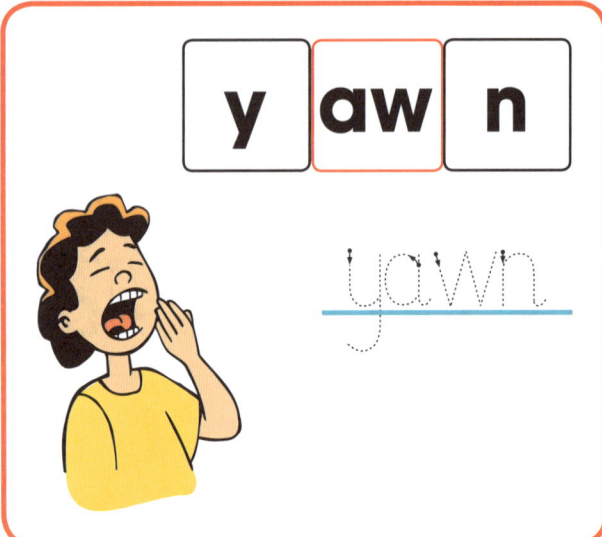

Read the rhyme

Circle **aw** in the rhyme.

We hammer and saw.

We paint and draw.

I pad on my paws.

I grip with my claws.

Read the words

Read the words. Write the words.

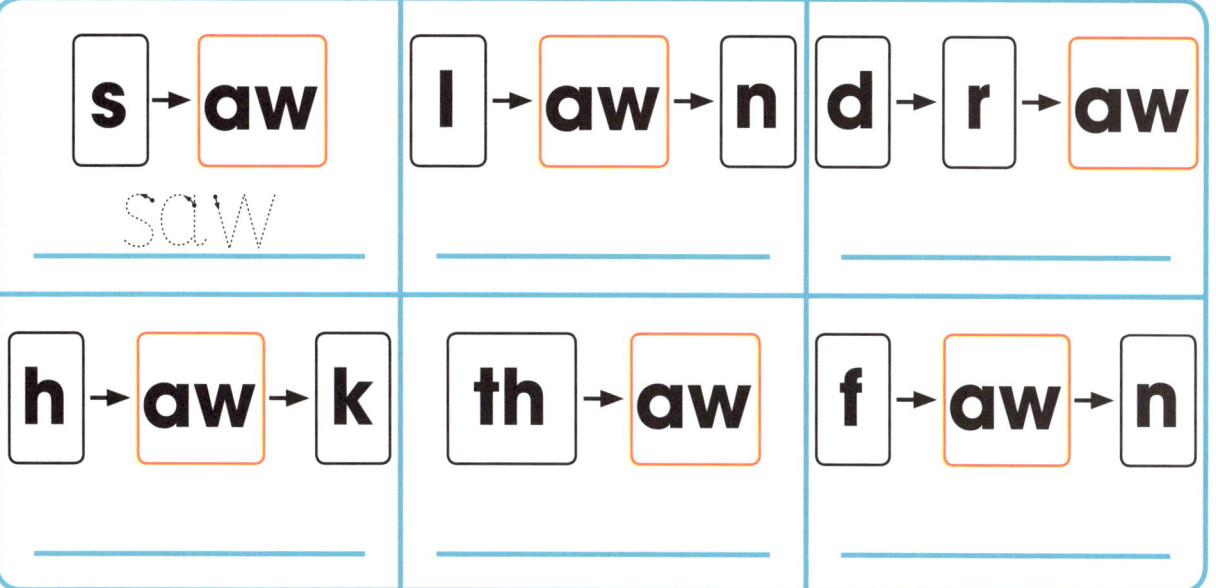

s → aw
saw

l → aw → n

d → r → aw

h → aw → k

th → aw

f → aw → n

Write the words

Write the correct word under each picture.

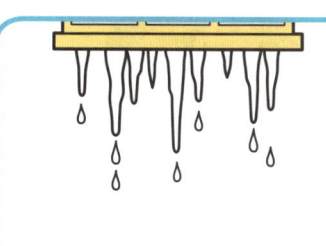

Words with ew

Read the rhyme

Circle **ew** in the rhyme.

I drew it!

I grew it!

I threw it!

Words with ew

Make the words

Make the words. Write the words. Read the words.

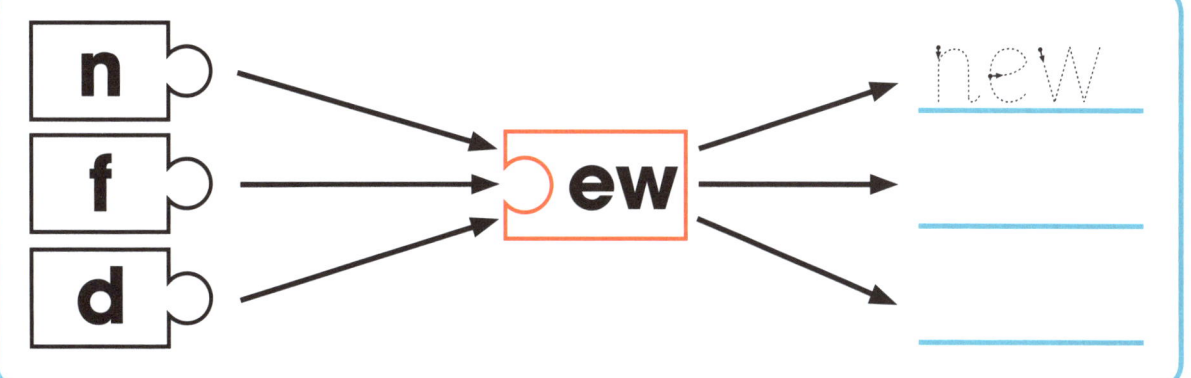

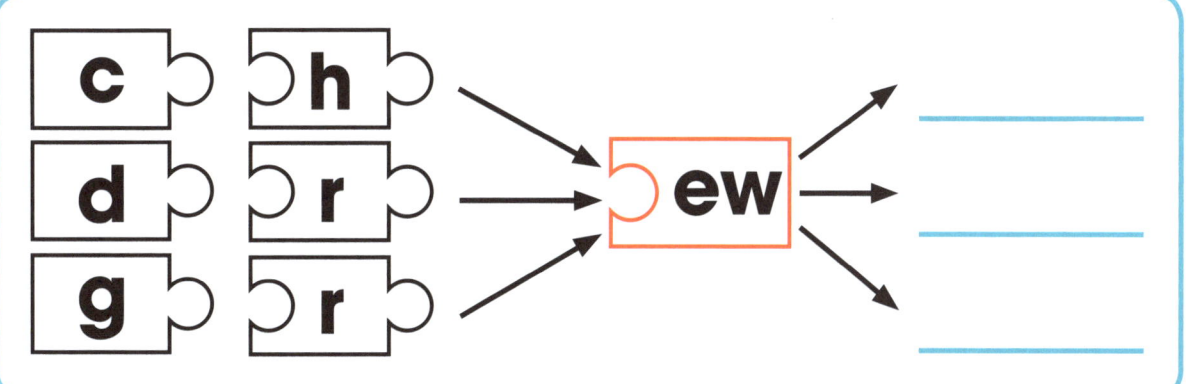

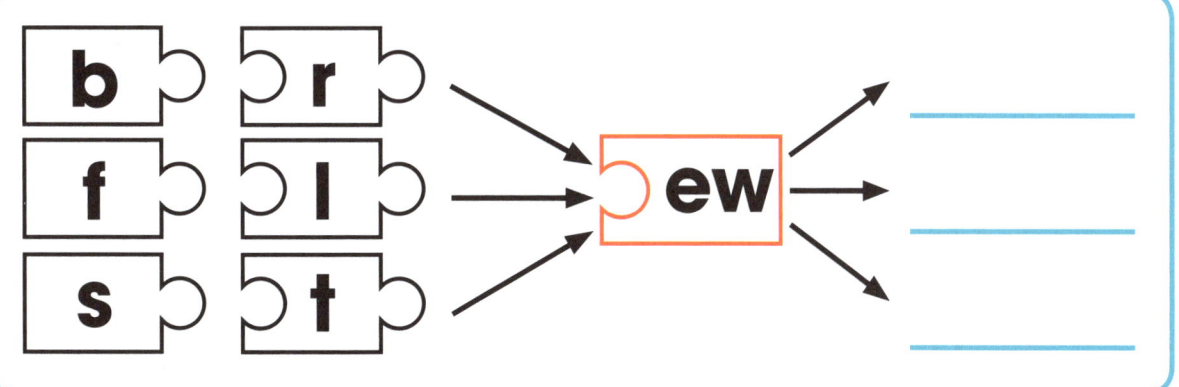

Parent's tip

If necessary, explain that there are different ways of spelling the same sound. Write 'ew' and ask your child to say the sound 'ew' and give some examples of words he/she has learned that have 'ew' in them. For example: chew, grew, flew, drew, threw.

Words with ue

Make the words

Make some words and names. Read the words.

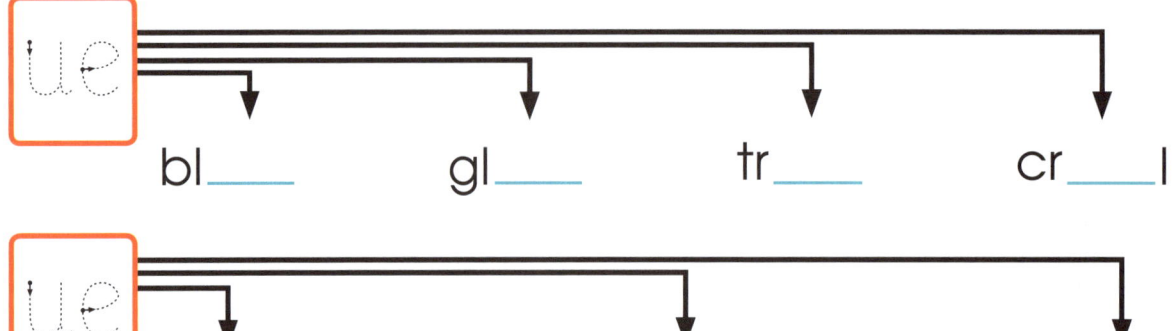

ue

bl____   gl____   tr____   cr____l

ue

T____sday   val____   resc____

Write the words

Write the words in the grid. Put one sound in each box.

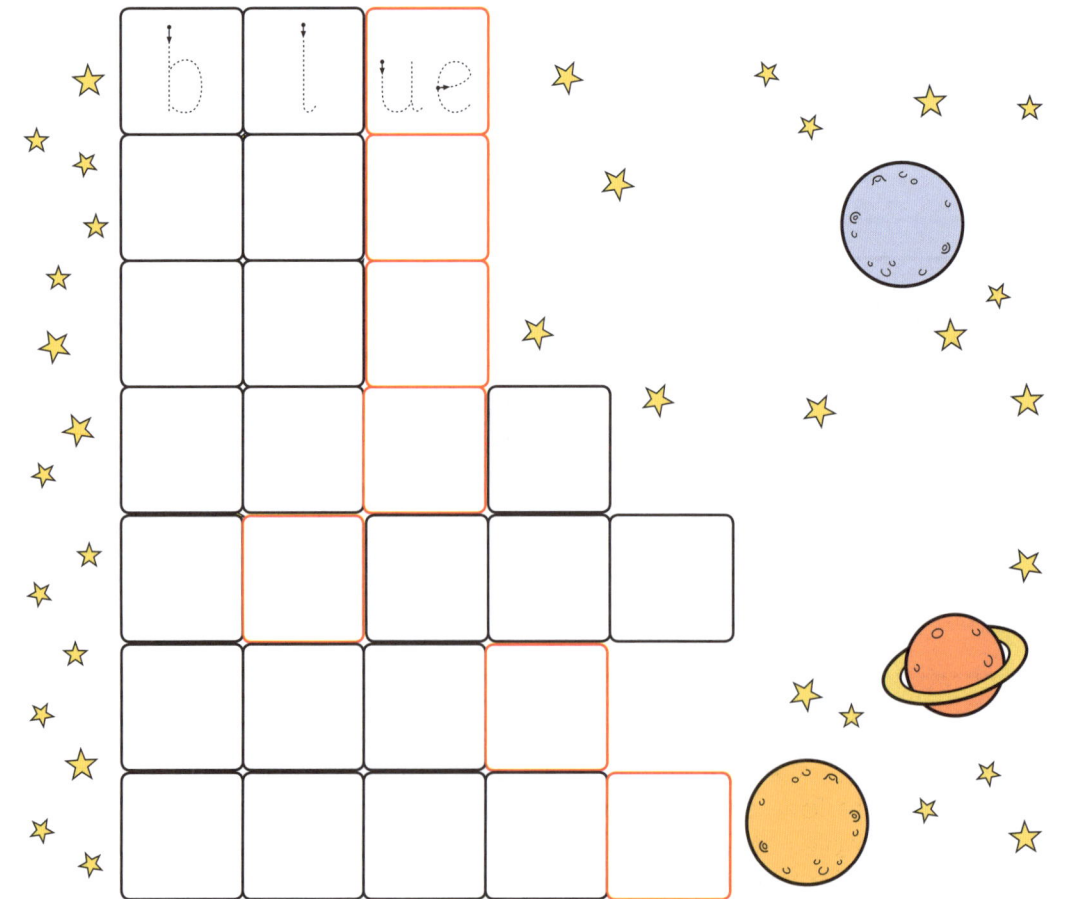

b | l | ue

Make the words

Make some words and names. Read the words.

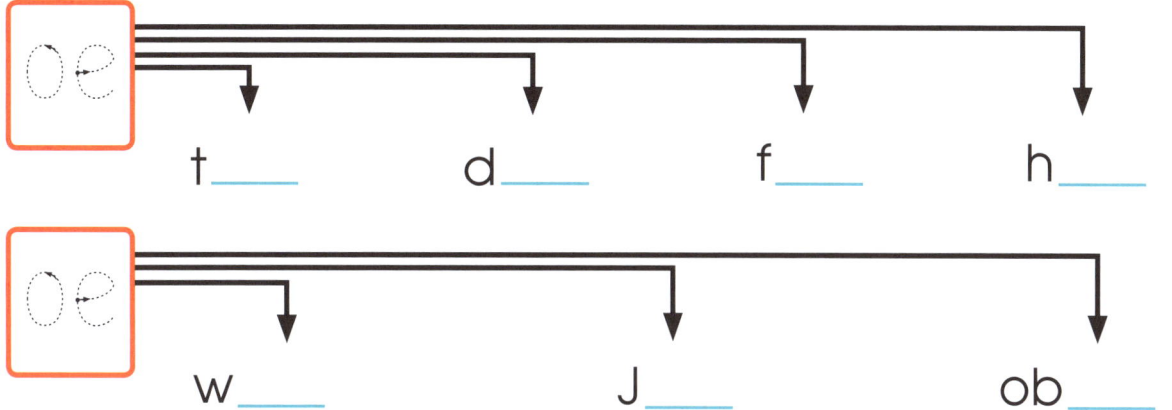

oe

t___   d___   f___   h___

oe

w___   J___   ob___

Write the words

Write the words in the grid. Put one sound in each box.

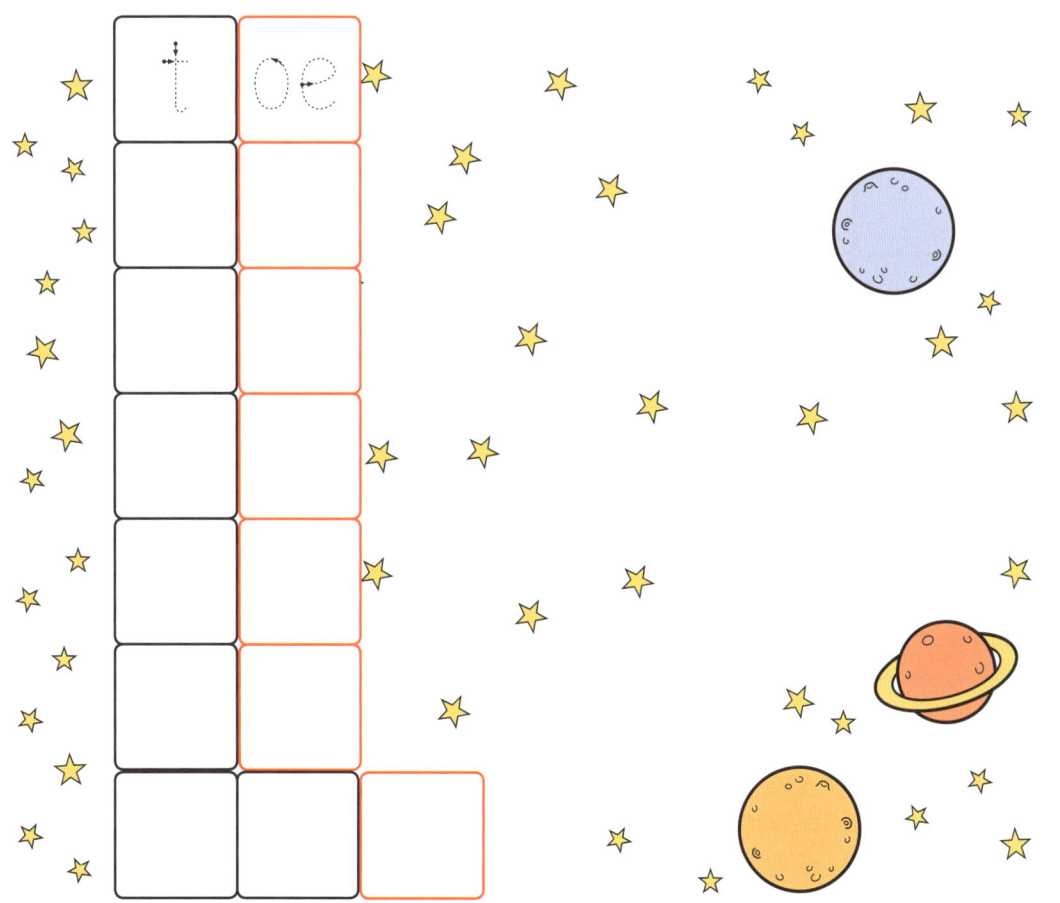

Words with au

Make the words

Make some words and names. Read the words.

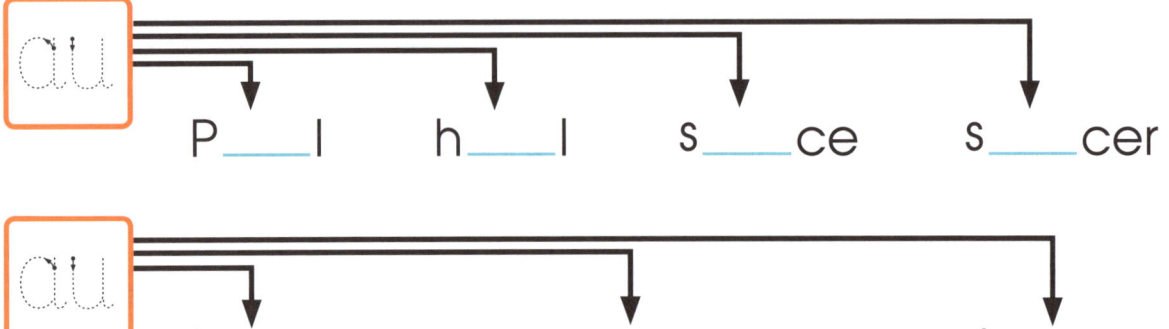

au

P__l   h___l   s___ce   s____cer

au

l___nch   ___gust   h___nt

Write the words

Write the words in the grid. Put one sound in each box.

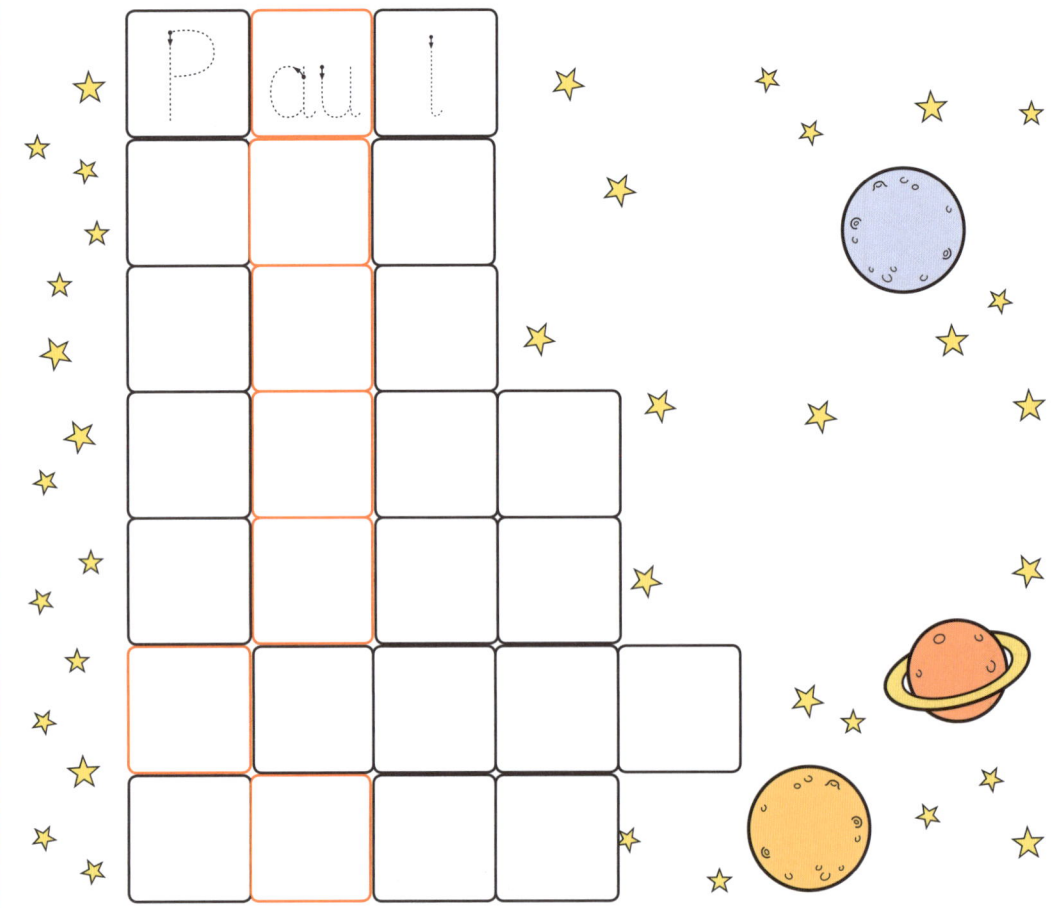

Make the words

Make some words with **ie**. Read the words.

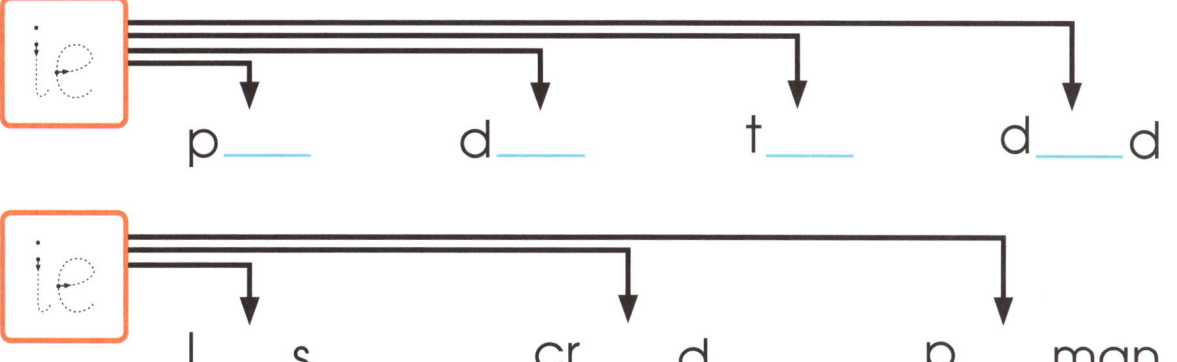

p____   d____   t____   d____d

l____s   cr____d   p____man

Write the words

Write the words in the grid. Put one sound in each box.

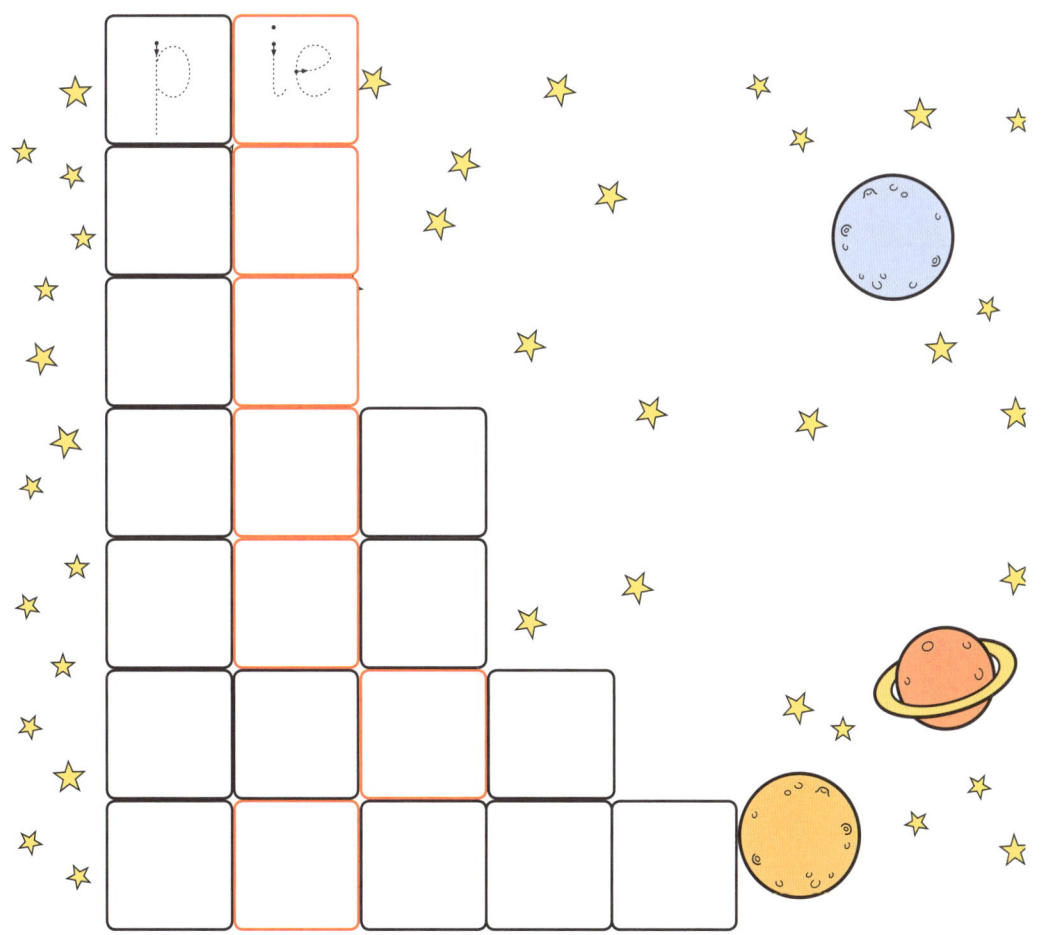

When ey says ay

Make some words

Make some words with **ey**. Read the words.

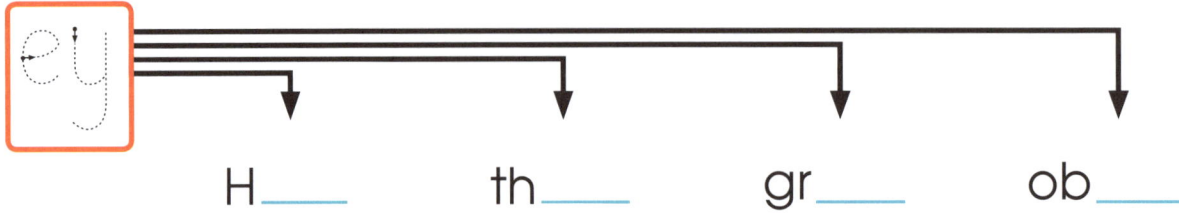

H_____   th_____   gr_____   ob_____

Hey! **ey** can say **ay**!

Write the words

Write the words in the grid. Put one sound in each box.

My nest is a dr____.

When ey says ee

Make the words

Make the words with **ey**.

Read the words. Write the words.

Split digraph a-e

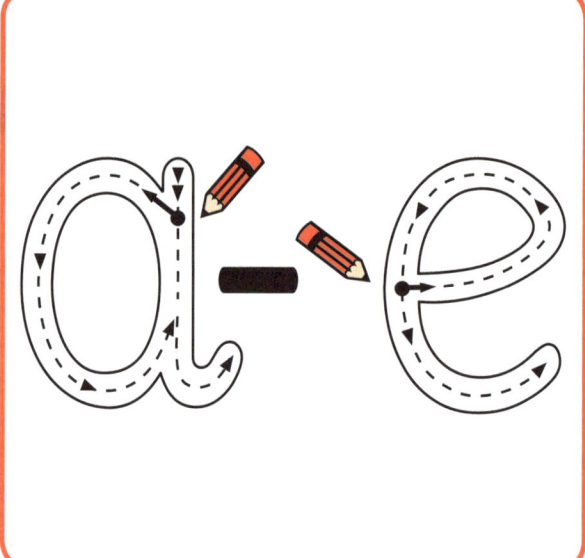

Read the story

Colour **a-e** in the story. Join **a-e**.

1 Wake up.

2 Make the bed.

3 Shake the mat.

4 Rake the leaves.

5 Bake a cake.

6 Take a nap!

Split digraph a͡-e

Write the words

Write the a͡-e words.

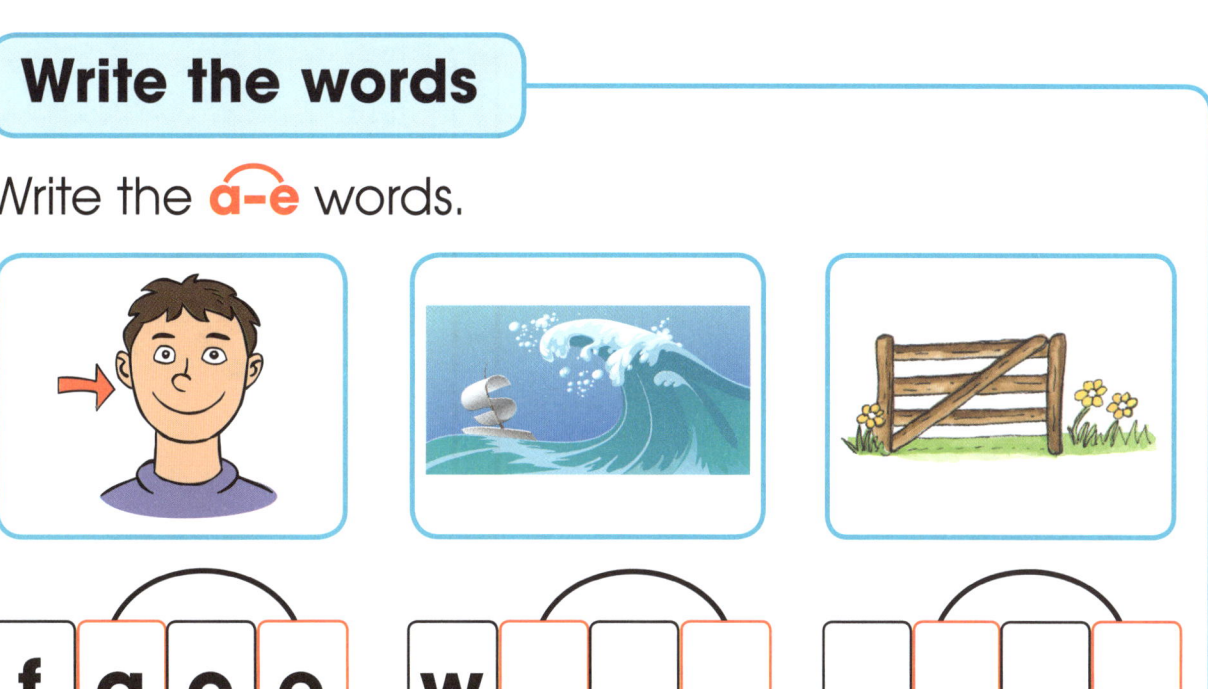

f	a	c	e

w			

Match the words

Match up the rhyming words.

Write the words.
Read the words.

Ladder 1:
made
gale
name
plate
lane
cave

Ladder 2:
sale
skate
spade
mane
save
tame

made spade

Split digraph i-e

s m i l e

smile

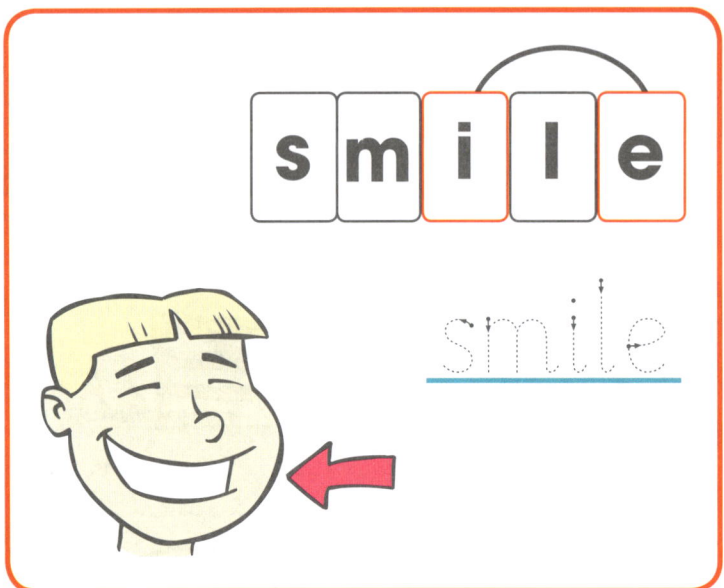

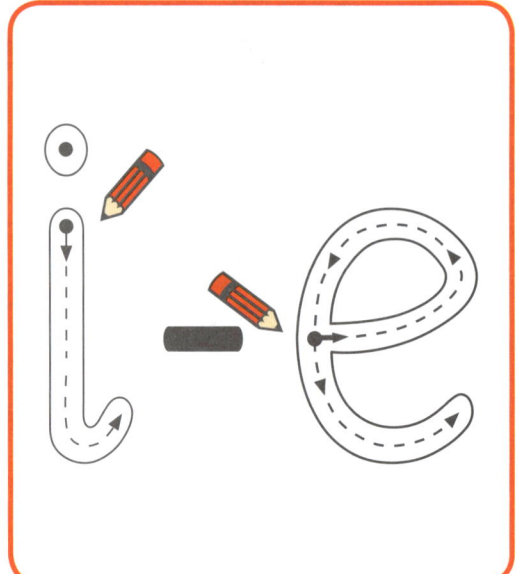

Read the rhyme

Colour **i-e** in the rhyme. Join **i-e**.

Sail down the Nile,
And after a mile
You will see a crocodile
With a fine smile!

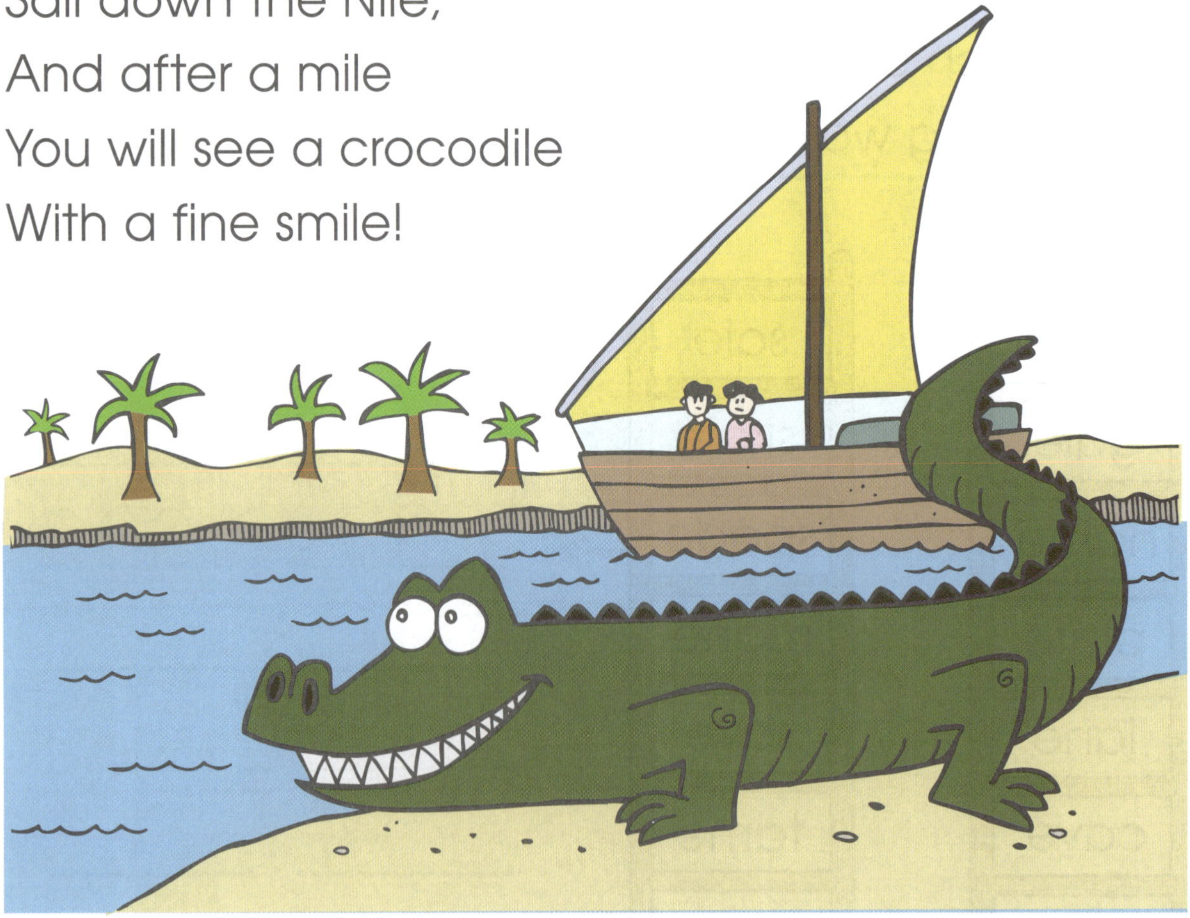

Split digraph i‑e

Write the words

Write the **i‑e** words.

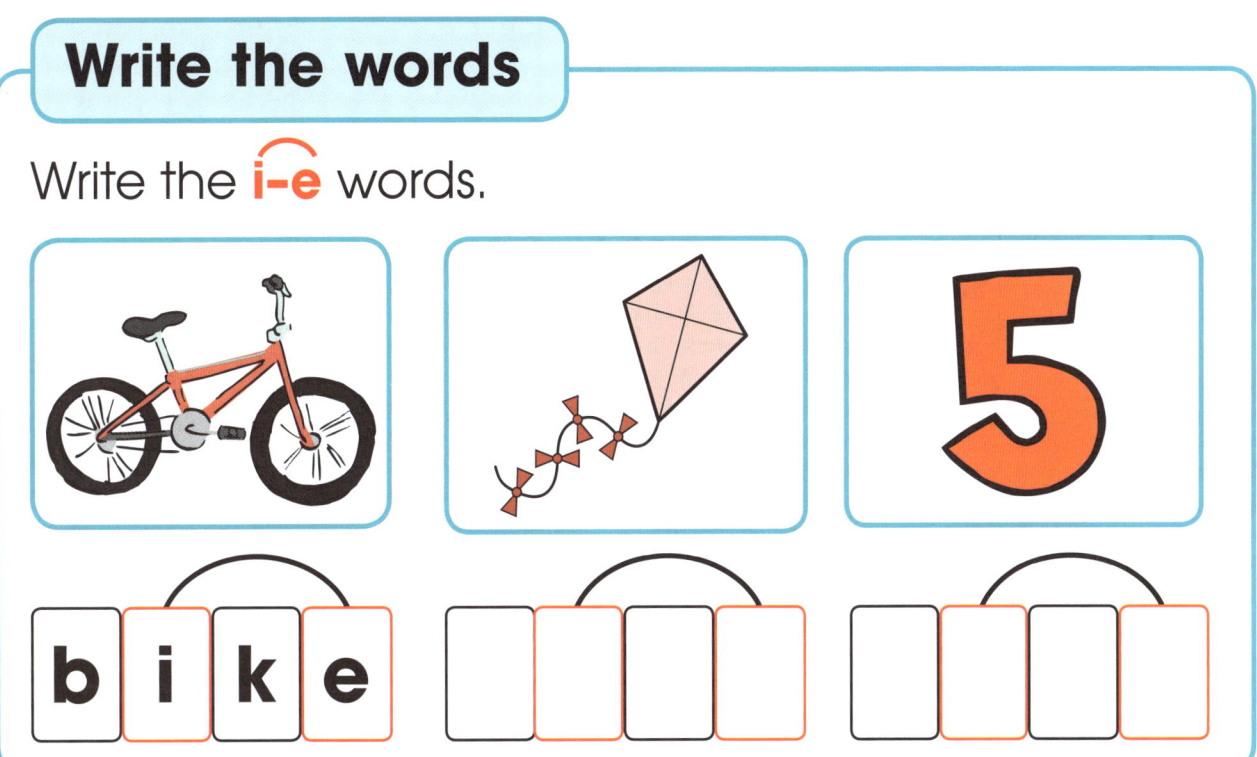

b	i	k	e

Match the words

Match up the rhyming words.

Write the words.
Read the words.

ride
like
time
wipe
rise
dive

spike
wise
stripe
hive
slide
chime

ride   slide

Split digraph o–e

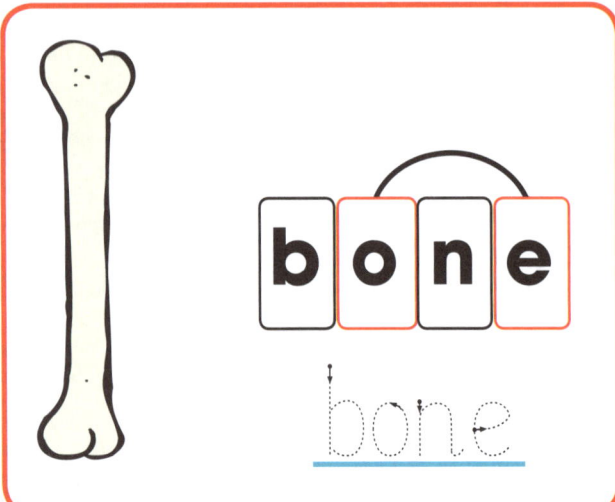

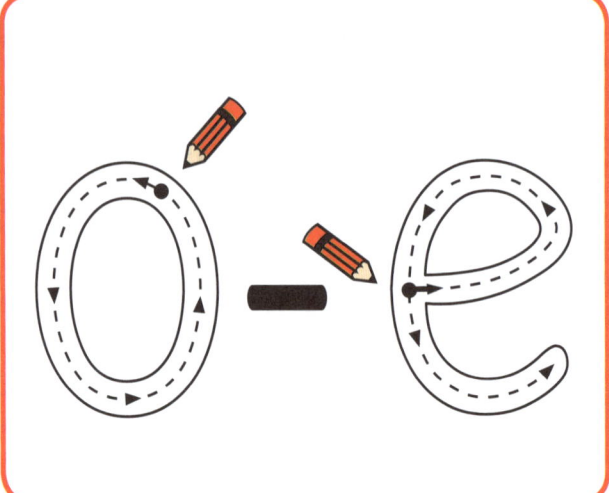

Read the rhyme

Colour **o–e** in the rhyme. Join **o–e**.

Old King Cole
Fell down a hole.
He broke a bone
On a big stone.

Write the words

Write the **o-e** words.

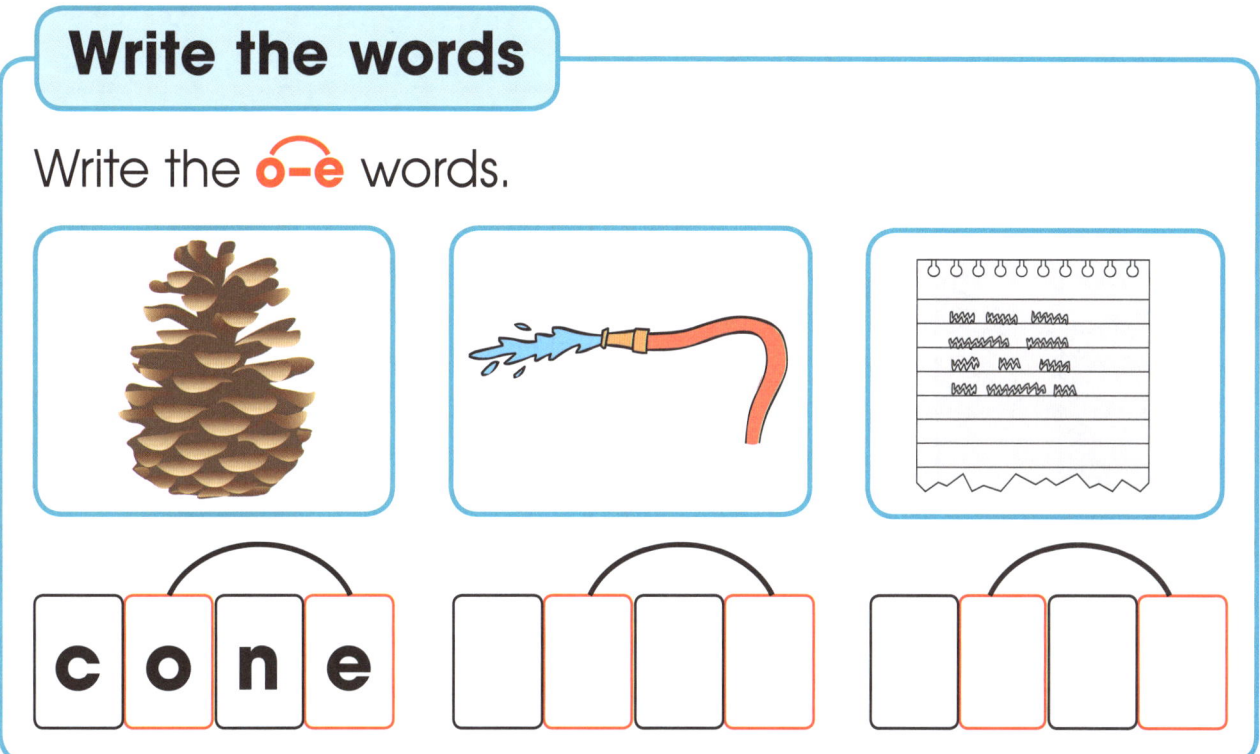

c	o	n	e

Match the words

Match up the rhyming words.

Write the words.
Read the words.

nose
joke
hope
bone
home
pole

rope
stole
dome
poke
close
stone

nose close

Split digraph u-e

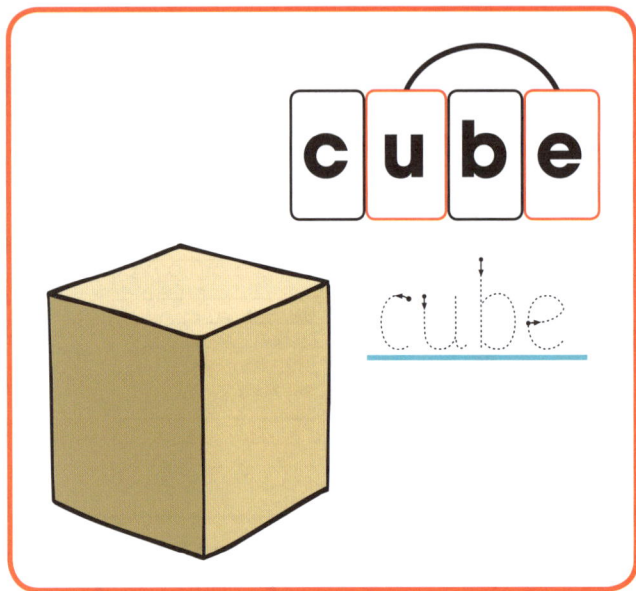

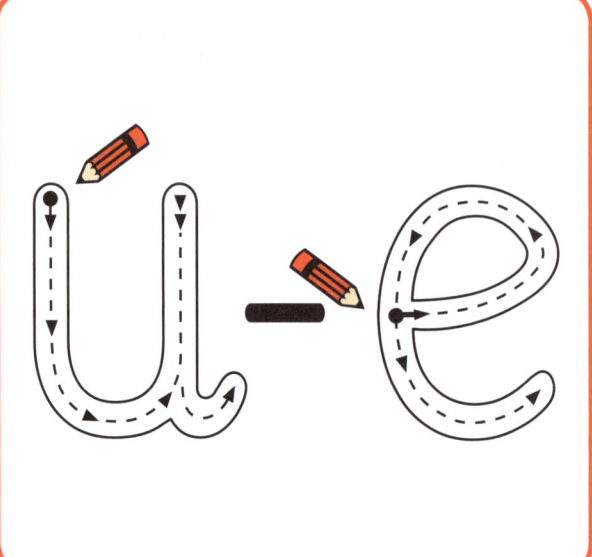

Read the rhyme

Colour **u-e** in the rhyme. Join **u-e**.

Duke Luke plays a tune on his flute.

Split digraph u–e

Write the words

Write the **u–e** words.

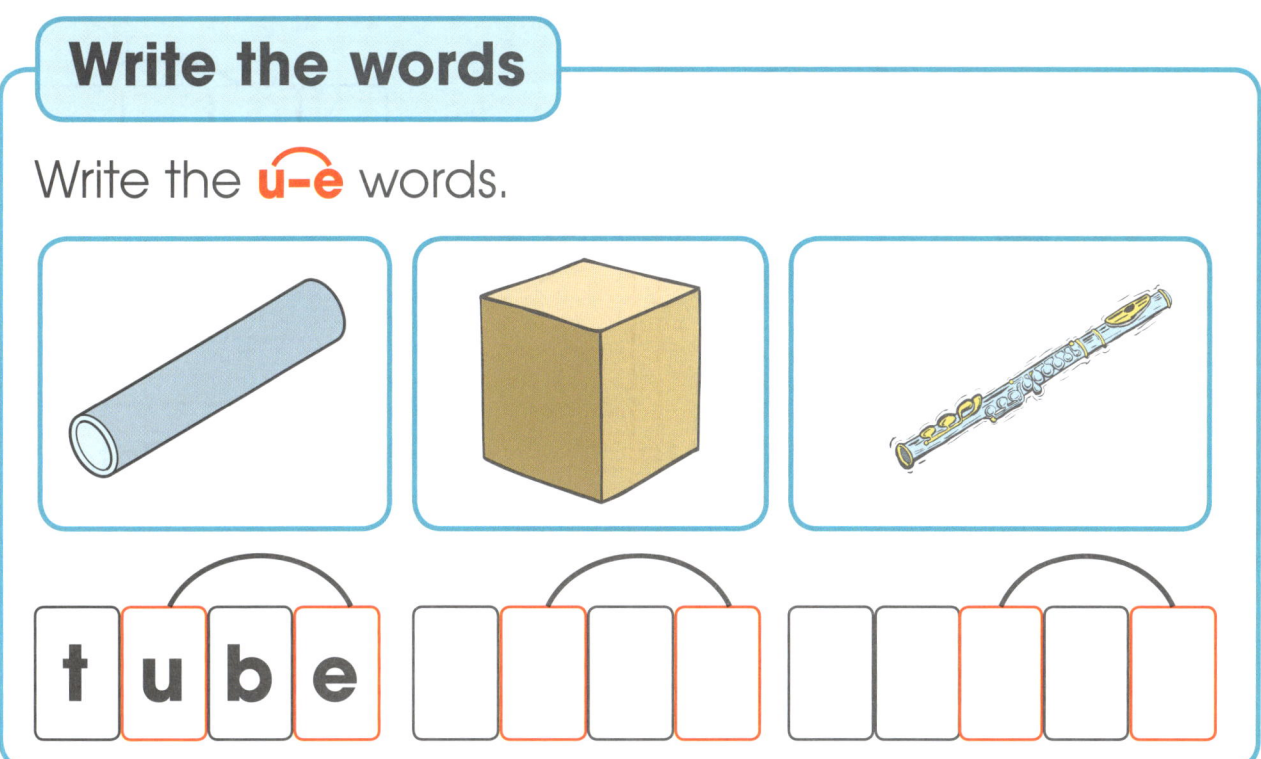

| t | u | b | e |

Match the words

Match up the rhyming words.

Write the words. Read the words.

cube
tune
rule
use
cute
duke

June
fuse
Luke
flute
tube
mule

cube   tube

Split digraph e-e

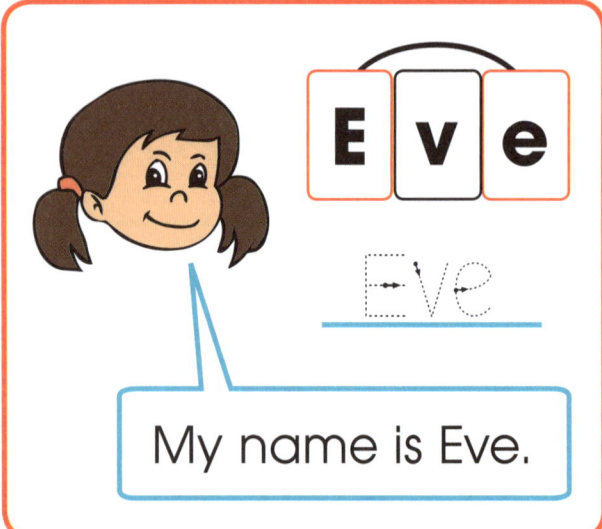

E v e

Eve

My name is Eve.

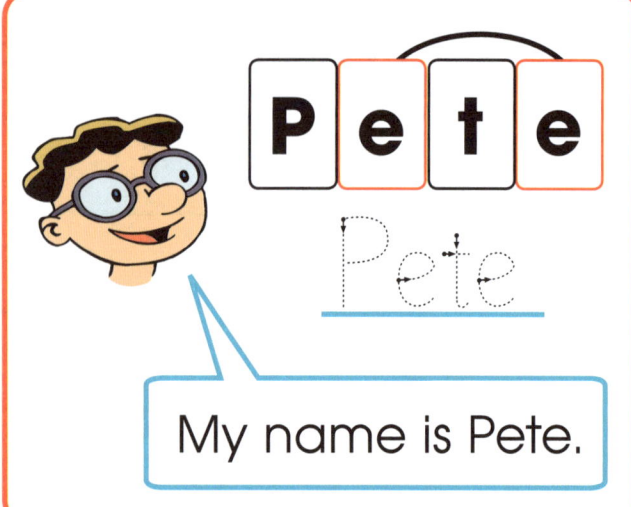

P e t e

Pete

My name is Pete.

Make the words

Make the words and names with **e-e**.
Read the words. Write the words.

th s → _____

th m → _____

S t v → _____

e x t r m → _____

c o n c r t → _____

Complete the words

Complete the words with **i**. Read the words.
Write the words.

| f | i | n | d | | m | | n | d | | b | | n | d |

_____ _____ _____

Make the words

Make the words with **i**.
Read the words. Write the words.

| ch | | l | d | → _____

| w | | l | d | → _____

| p | | n | t | → _____

| k | | n | d | → _____

| b | e | h | | n | d | → _____

When a says ar

Write the word

Write the word for each picture. Read the words.

r a f t

m

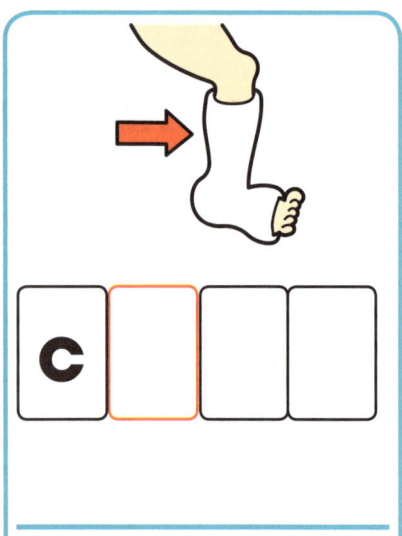

c

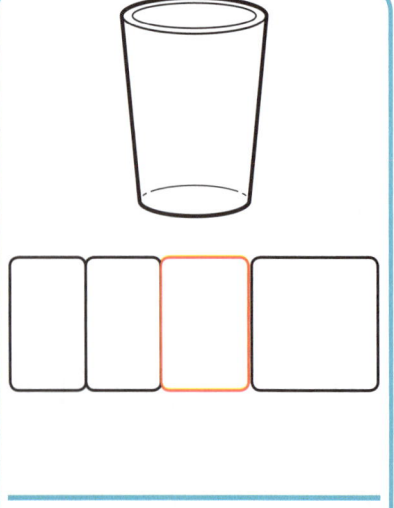

a c or n

acorn

Make the words

Make the words with **a**.

Read the words. Write the words.

| p | r | o | n | → _____ |

| p | r | i | l | → _____ |

b | s | i | n | → _____ |

J | s | o | n | → _____ |

| p | r | i | c | o | t | → _____ |

A different u sound

Read the rhyme

Circle **u** in the rhyme.

Never pull or push

A bull in a bush.

For if you do,

It may push you, too!

Parent's tip This page is not appropriate where the regional pronunciation is 'u' as in 'cup'.

A different u sound

Choose the word

Choose the correct word for each picture.

full	pull

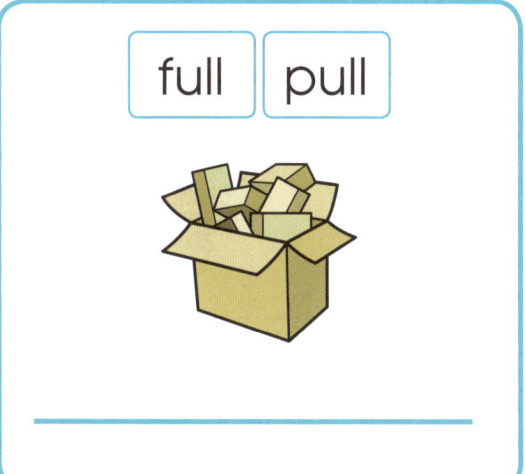

_____

pull	bull

_____

bush	push

_____

push	put

_____

bull	bush

_____

pull	push

_____

When o says u

Write the words

Write the word for each picture.
They all rhyme.

love _____   _d_____   _____

Match the words

Match the rhyming words.	Write the words. Read the words.

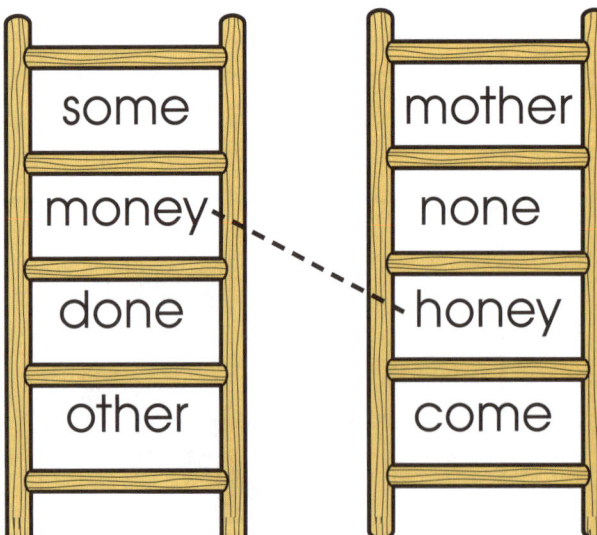

some   mother
money   none
done   honey
other   come

Write the name of a day
of the week with **o**.

_____ _____

_____ _____

_____ _____

_____ _____

_____

When er rhymes with her

| p | er | m |

perm

| f | er | n |

fern

Make the words

Make the words with **er**.

Read the words. Write the words.

| j | | k | ⟶ _____
| t | | m | ⟶ _____
| k | | b | ⟶ _____
| s | t | | n | ⟶ _____
| p | | ch | ⟶ _____

When ow says oh

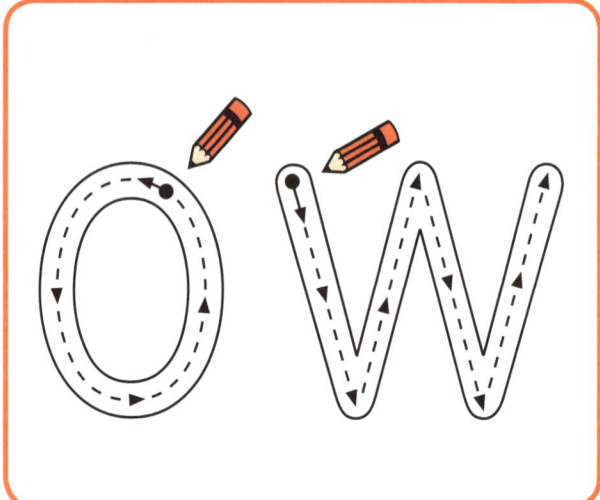

Read the rhyme

Circle **ow** in the rhyme.

I can row.

I can mow.

I can blow.

I can grow!

Parent's tip Your child might know words in which 'ow' represents the 'ow' sound in 'cow'. Point out that 'ow' can be used for a different sound – in glow, show, grow, snow and many other words.

Swop the sound

Read the words.	Swap the first sound for:	Write the words. Read the words.
low	m	mow
tow	r	
crow	g	
blow	s	
glow	f	
grow	c	
follow	h	
borrow	s	
yellow	b	
pillow	w	
narrow	b	

When ie says ee

Write the words

Write the words with **ie**. Read the words.

| ch | ie | f | | th | ie | f | | b | r | ie | f |

_____ _____ _____

Make the words

Make the words with **ie**.
Read the words. Write the words.

| f | | l | d | → _____

| sh | | l | d | → _____

| p | r | | s | t | → _____

| sh | r | | k | → _____

| b | e | l | | f | → _____

When y says ee

j	e	ll	y

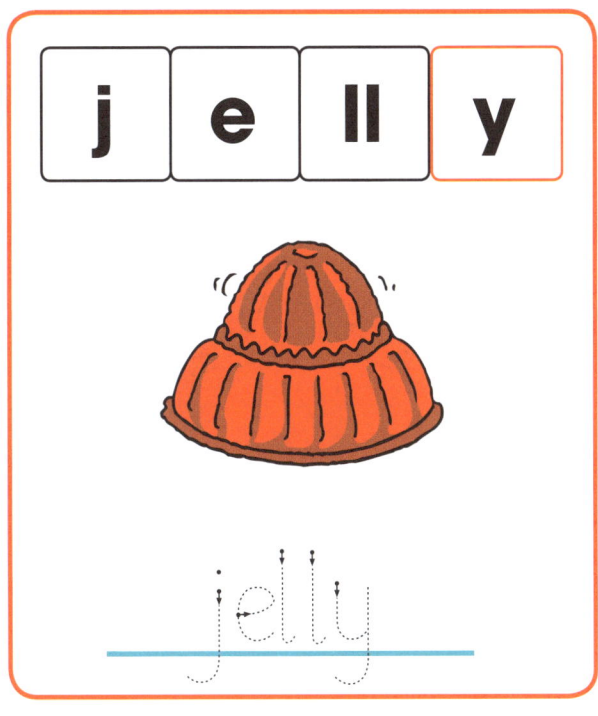

jelly

m	u	mm	y

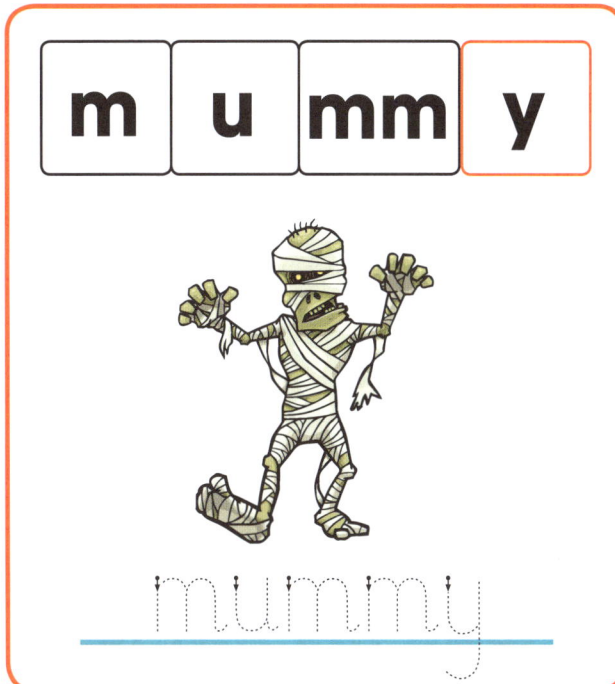

mummy

Make the words

Make the words with **y**.

Read the words. Write the words.

h	o	ll	

→ _____

l	a	z	

→ _____

h	a	pp	

→ _____

oi	l	

→ _____

e	v	er	

→ _____

When ea says e

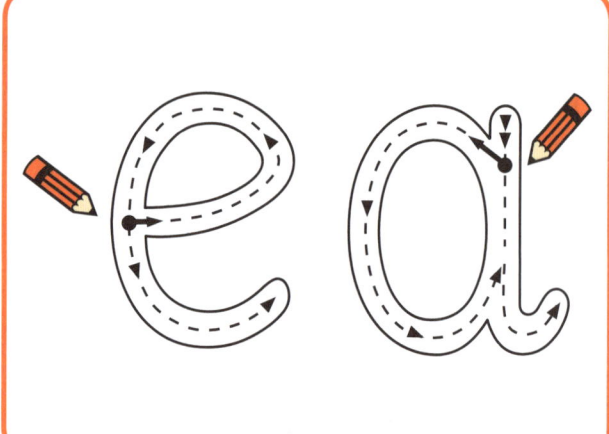

Read the rhyme

Circle **ea** in the rhyme.

The little bird is pecking for bread.

Bob, bob, bob goes its head.

It flaps its wings and shakes its feathers.

It visits my garden in all kinds of weather.

Swop the sound

Read the words.	Swap the first sound for:	Write the words.
head	d	dead
bread	d	
thread	s p	
feather	w	
leather	h	
ready	s t	
healthy	w	
death	b r	

Parent's tip Your child might know words in which 'ea' represents the 'ea' sound (like ee) in 'meat'. Point out that 'ea' can be used for a different sound – in dead, bread, head, deaf and many other words.

When y says igh

cry

cry

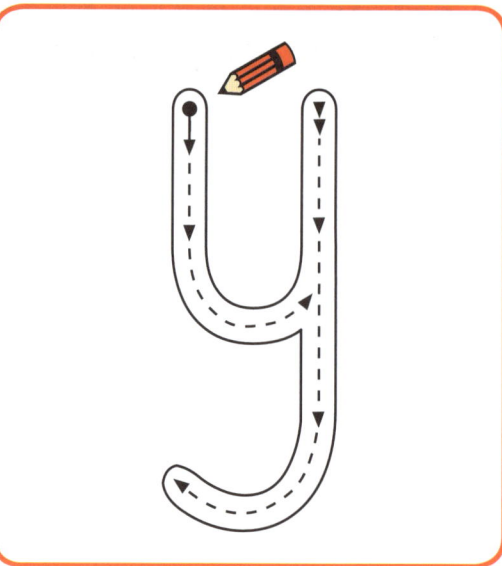

Read the rhyme

Circle **y** in the rhyme.

Why do you cry? Why do you cry?
Soon you'll be a butterfly.
And flutter by in the sky!

When y says igh

Make the words

Make the **y** words.

Read the words. Write the words.

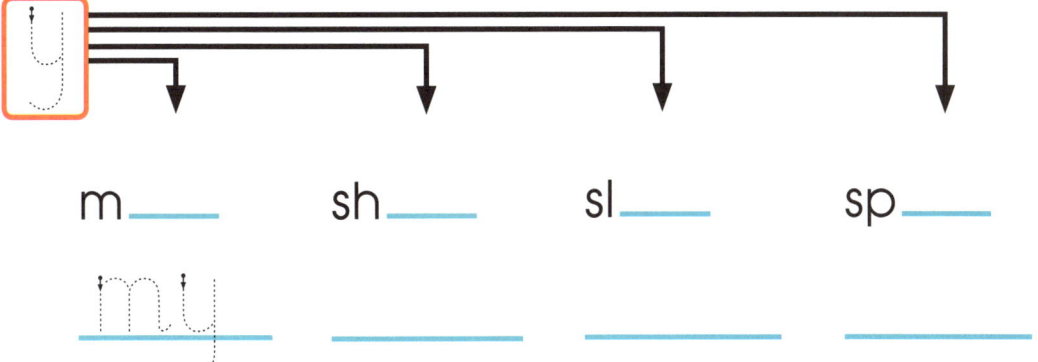

m_____   sh_____   sl_____   sp_____

my   _____   _____   _____

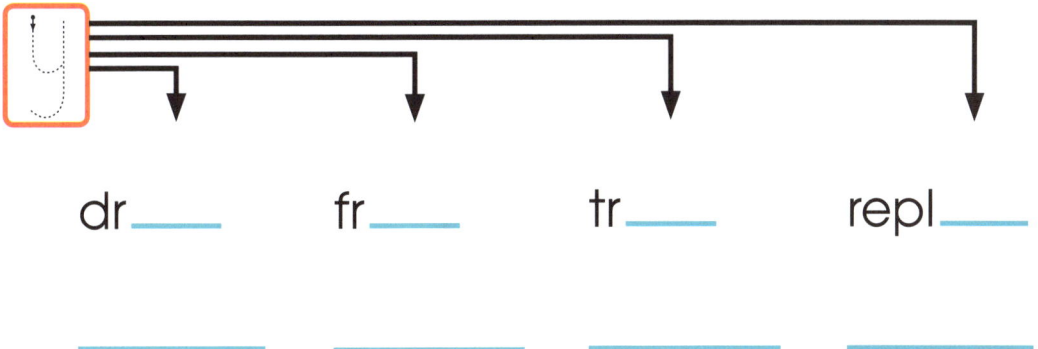

dr_____   fr_____   tr_____   repl_____

_____   _____   _____   _____

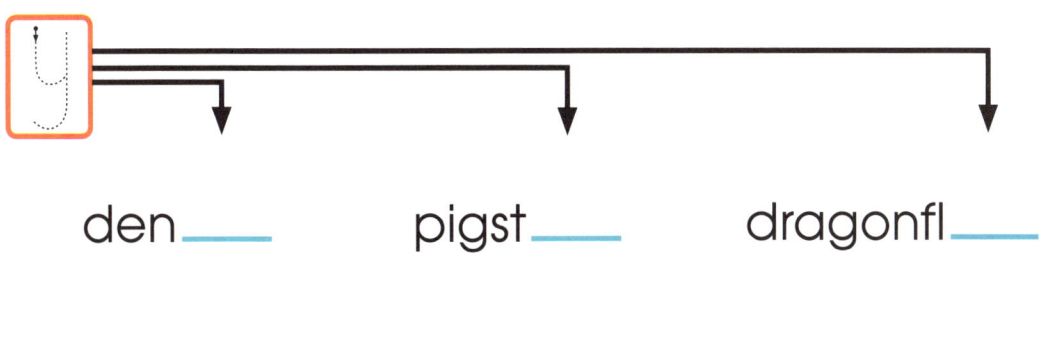

den_____   pigst_____   dragonfl_____

_____   _____   _____

When or says ur

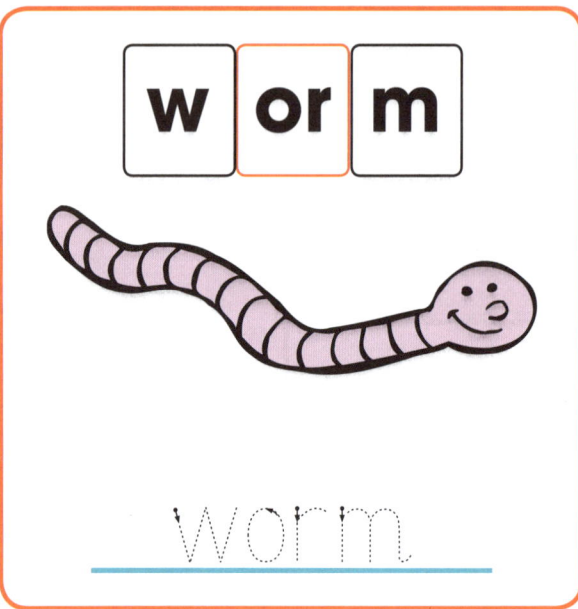

worm

world

Make the words

Make the words with **or**.

Read the words. Write the words.

| w | | d | → _____ |

| w | | k | → _____ |

| w | | th | → _____ |

| w | | s | t | → _____ |

| w | | sh | i | p | → _____ |

p	al	m

palm

al	m	o	n	d

almond

Make the words

Make the words with **al**.

Read the words. Write the words.

c		f

→ _____

h		f

→ _____

c		m

→ _____

l	i	p	b		m

→ _____

When ear says er

b ear

bear

ear

Read the rhyme

Circle **ear** in the rhyme.

Teddy bear, teddy bear,

Your coat has a tear.

Teddy bear, teddy bear,

What will you wear?

Make the words

Make some words.

Write the words.

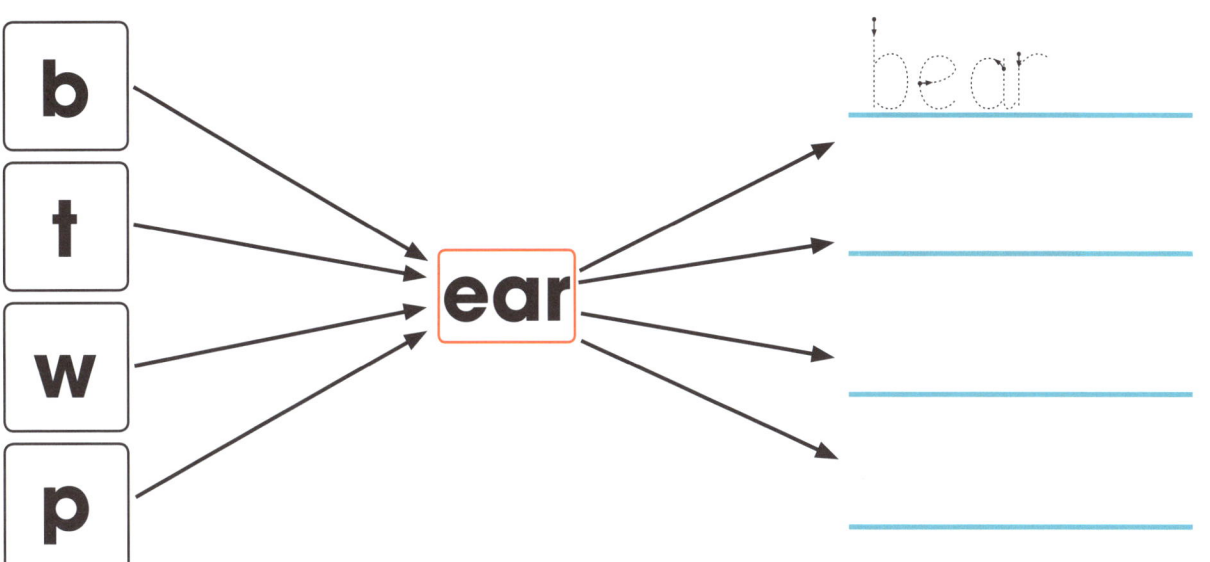

b

t

w

p

ear

bear

Use the words to fill in the crossword.

Down

1. A large wild animal
2. To dress in something

Across

3. A kind of fruit
4. To rip something

When are says air

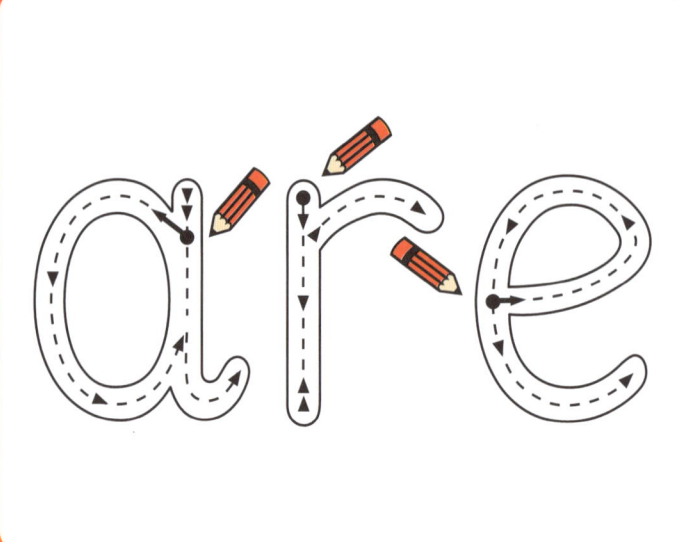

Read the rhyme

Circle **are** in the rhyme.

Once I saw a rare hare.

"Stare at me if you dare," said the hare.

"I don't care!"

I have stares to spare.

Make the words

Make some words with **are**. Read the words.
Write the words.

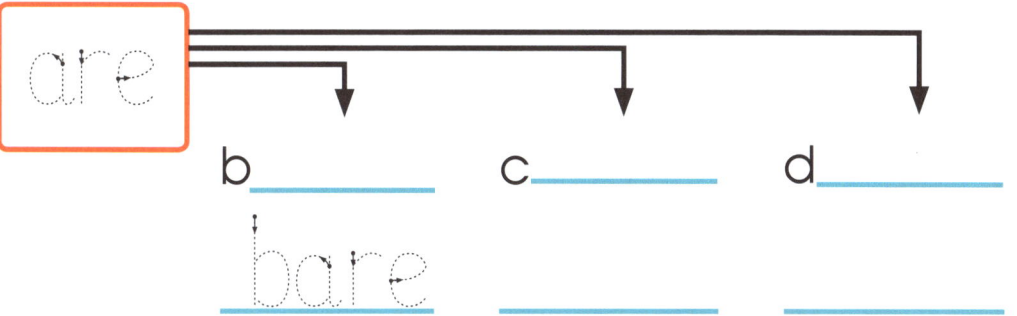

are → b_____ c_____ d_____

bare _____ _____

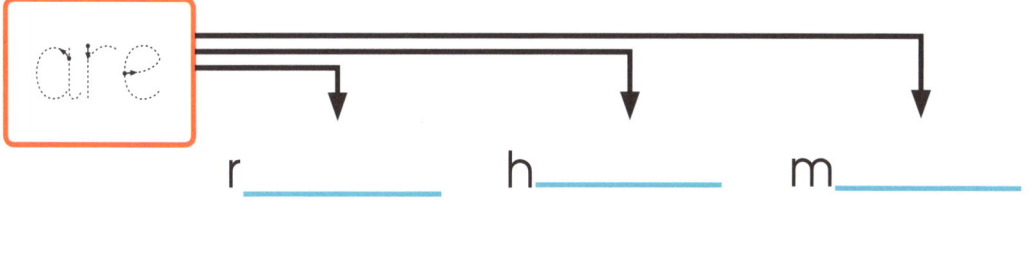

are → r_____ h_____ m_____

_____ _____ _____

are → sh_____ sc_____ sp_____

_____ _____ _____

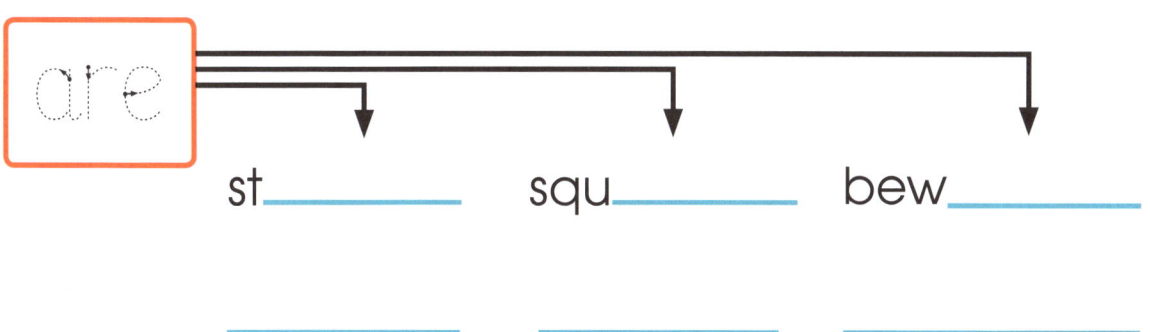

are → st_____ squ_____ bew_____

_____ _____ _____

Words with eer

d **eer**

deer

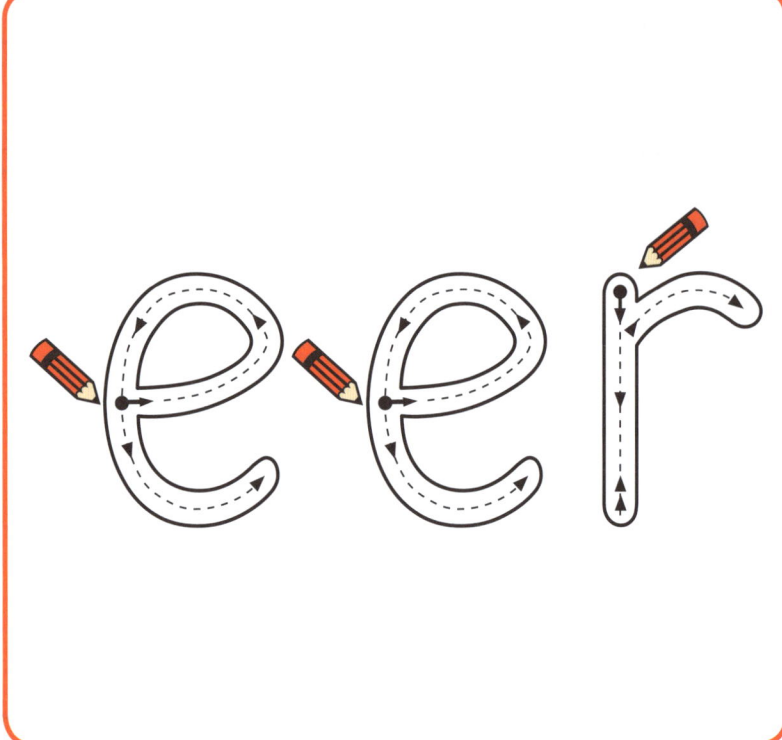

Make the words

Make the words with **eer**.

Read the words. Write the words.

j  ⟶ _____

p  ⟶ _____

sh  ⟶ _____

s **t**  ⟶ _____

Parent's tip Practise saying the 'eer' sound in 'deer' with your child. Explain that all the words have this sound and that even if your child hasn't seen or heard these words before he/she can read them by sounding the letters.

Sort the words

Read the words.

Sort the words into sets.

ear words	**eer** words

Words with oor

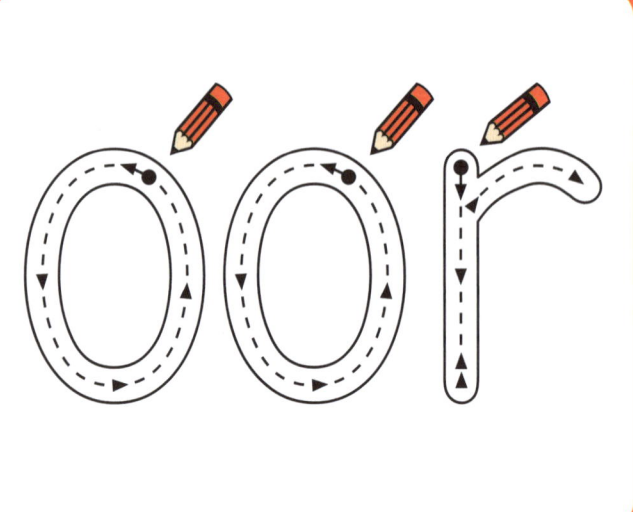

Make the words

Make the words with **oor**.

Read the words. Write the words.

d		→ _____
m		→ _____
p		→ _____
f	l		→ _____
t	a	n	d		i	→ _____

Join the words

Make words from door + another word.
Write the words.

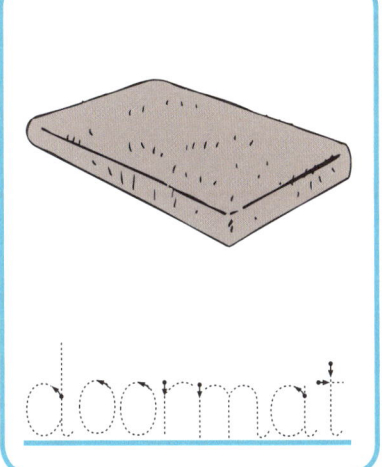

doormat

_____man

_____way

_____bell

_____step

trap_____

Parent's tip

Point out to your child that they have learned different ways of spelling the sound 'or'. Revisit page 64 and ask your child to read the word at the top of the page. Ask which letters spell the sound 'or'.

Tell your child that the words on this page have 'oor' in them. When your child has written the words, ask him/her to read them.

Words with ore

Read the rhyme

Circle **ore** in the rhyme.

Snore! Snore! Snore!
I can't stand any more.
I've told Dad before
That his snore is a bore!

Make the words

Make some words with **ore**. Read the words.

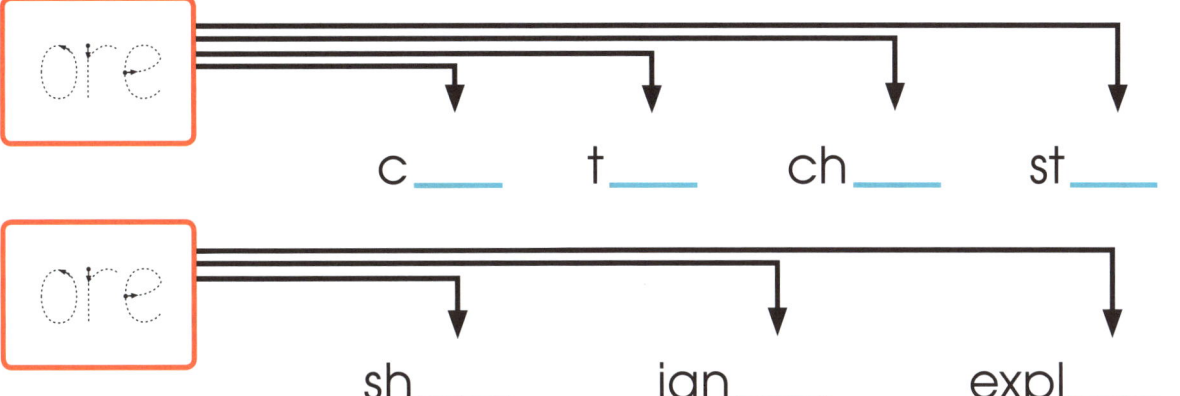

ore

c_____   t_____   ch_____   st_____

ore

sh_____   ign_____   expl_____

Write the words

Write the words in the grid. Put one sound in
each box.

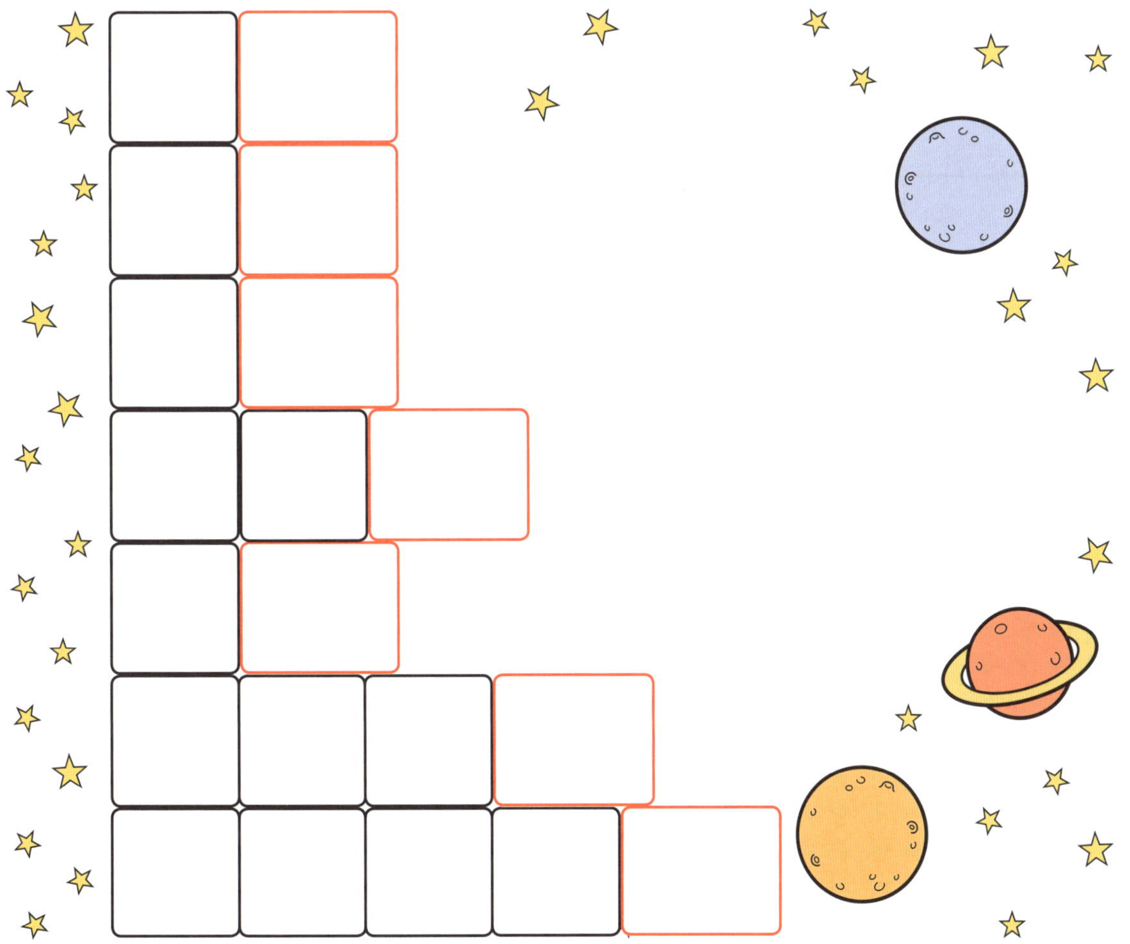

Words with our

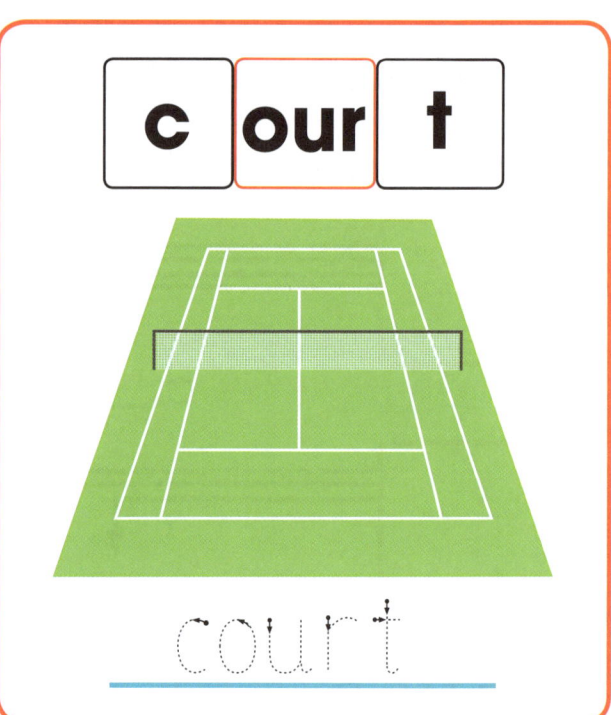

Make the words

Make the words with **our**.

Read the words. Write the words.

y		→ _____
f		→ _____
f		th	→ _____
f		t	ee	n	→ _____
c		t	y	ar	d	→ _____

d	augh	t	er

daughter

Make the words

Make the words with **augh**.

Read the words. Write the words.

d		t	er	→ _____

n		t	y	→ _____

c		t		→ _____

t		t		→ _____

s	l		t	er	→ _____

Words with al

w | al | k

walk

t | al | k

talk

Make the words

Make the words with **al**.
Read the words. Write the words.

ch | | k → _____

s | t | | k → _____

w | | k | er → _____

b | ea | n | s | t | | k → _____

s | i | d | e | w | | k → _____

Words with all

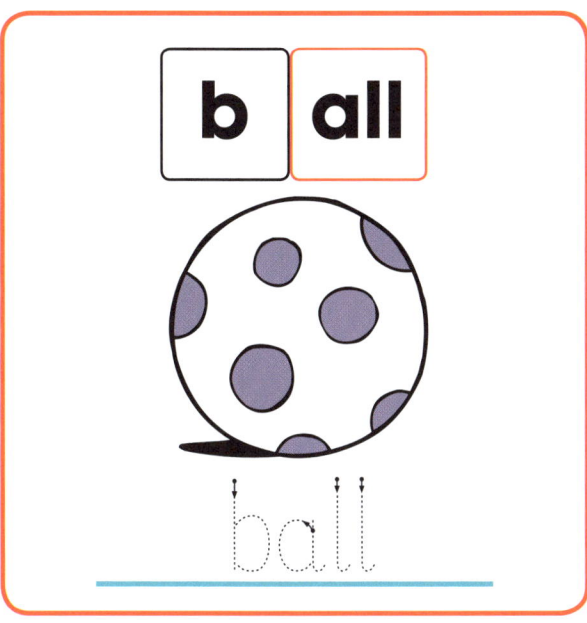

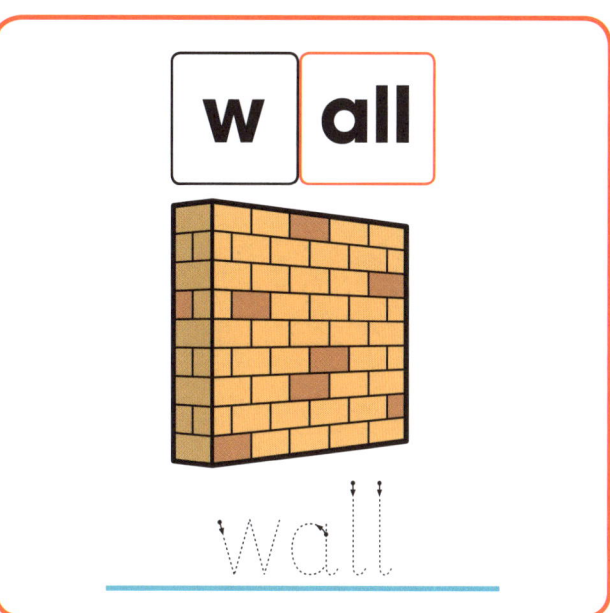

Make the words

Make the words with **all**.

Read the words. Write the words.

71

Words with wh

Read the words

Read the words that begin **wh**. Circle **wh** in the words.

Write two questions:

When _____

Why _____

Make the words

Make some words with **wh**. Write the words.
Read the words.

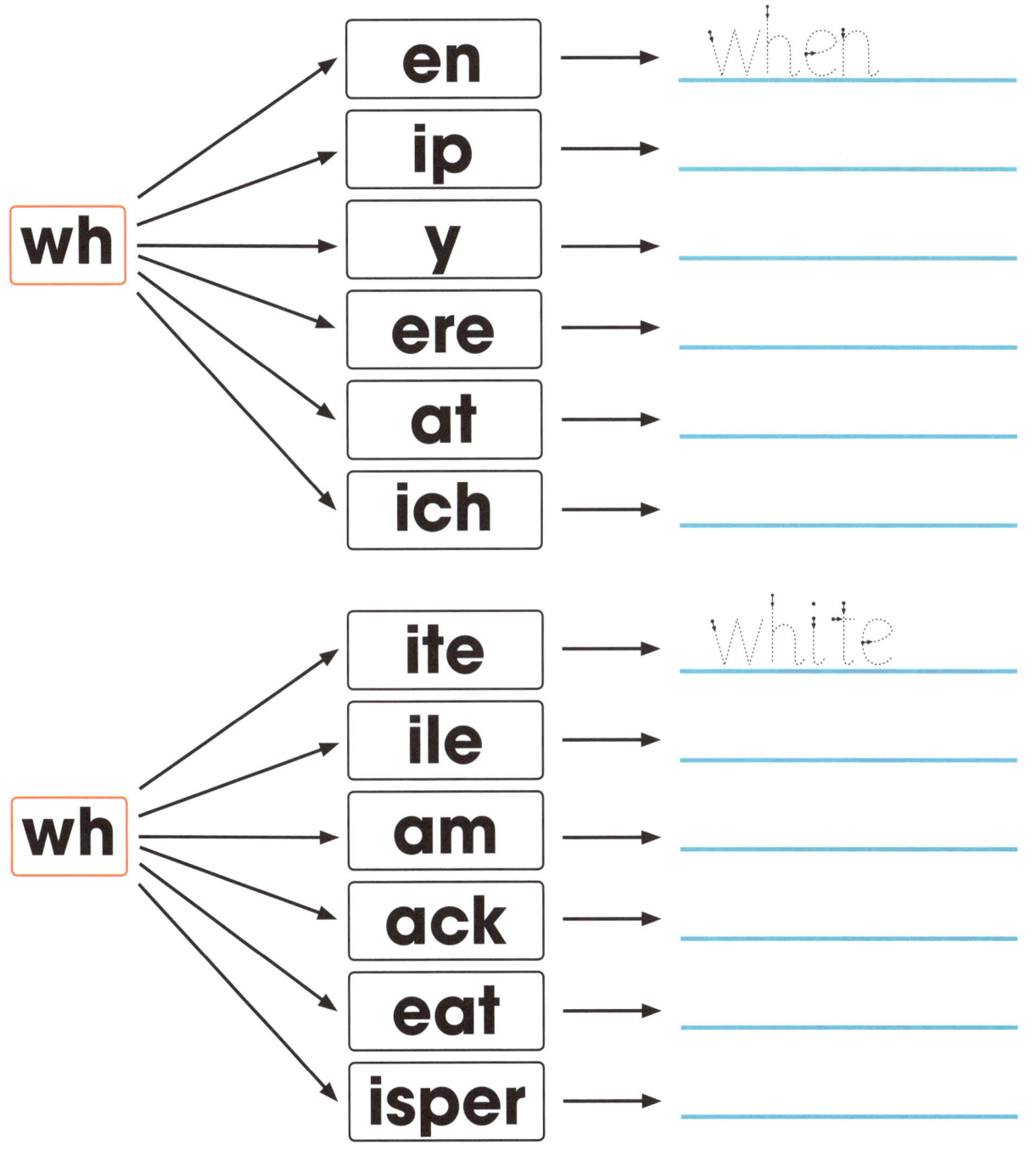

wh → en → *when*

wh → ip →

wh → y →

wh → ere →

wh → at →

wh → ich →

wh → ite → *white*

wh → ile →

wh → am →

wh → ack →

wh → eat →

wh → isper →

Parent's tip Ask your child which letter to use for the sound 'w' (say the sound, not the letter name). He/she should know that the letter is 'w'. Then ask if he/she knows how to spell 'when'. If so, point out the letters 'wh'. Tell him/her that there are a few words that have 'wh' for the 'w' sound.

Words with ph

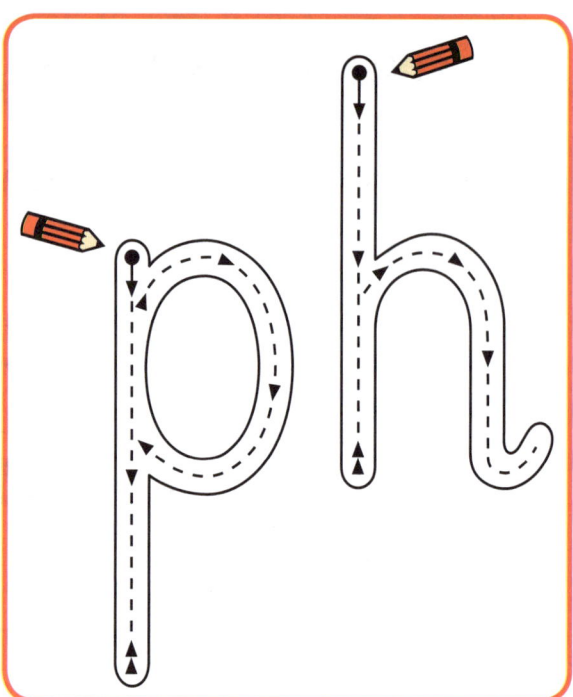

Read the rhyme

Circle **ph** in the rhyme.

We call the alphabet the ABC.

Elephants eat leaves from a tree.

Dolphins swim in the deep blue sea.

All my friends phone me!

Make the words

Make some words with **ph**. Read the words.
Write the words.

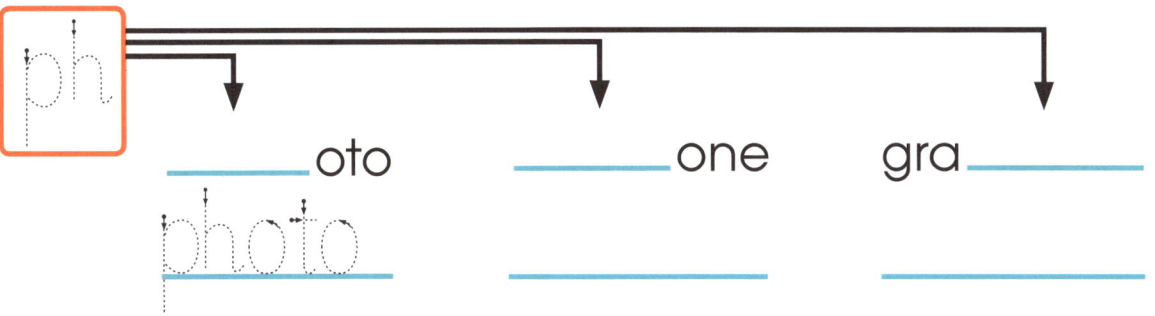

ph → _____oto   _____one   gra_____

photo   _____   _____

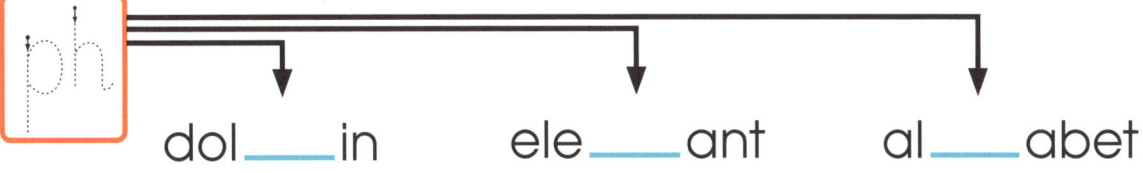

ph → dol_____in   ele_____ant   al_____abet

_____   _____   _____

Write the words

Write the correct word under each picture.

_____

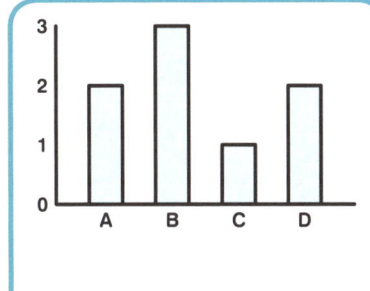

_____

_____

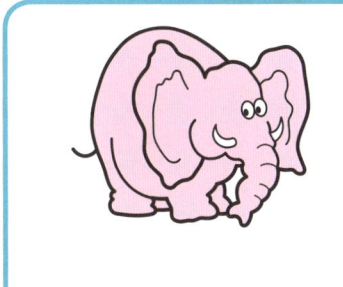

_____

_____

_____

Words with tch

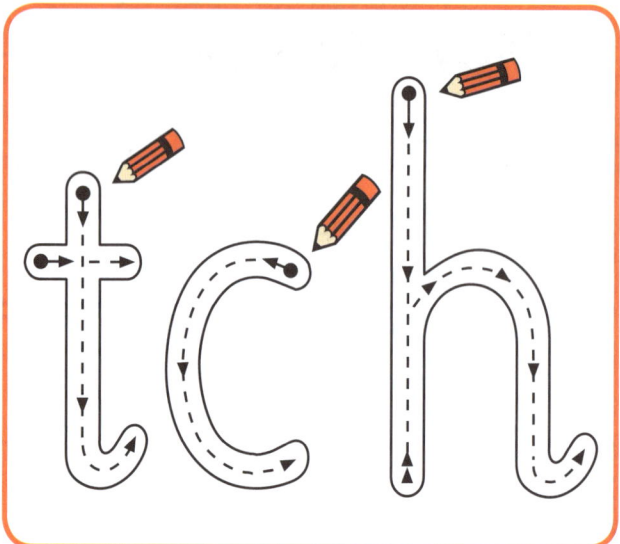

Read the rhyme

Circle **tch** in the rhyme.

We're all at the match.
See that catch!
Bowling down the pitch.
Oh, no! He's in the ditch!

Make the words

Make some words with **tch**. Read the words.

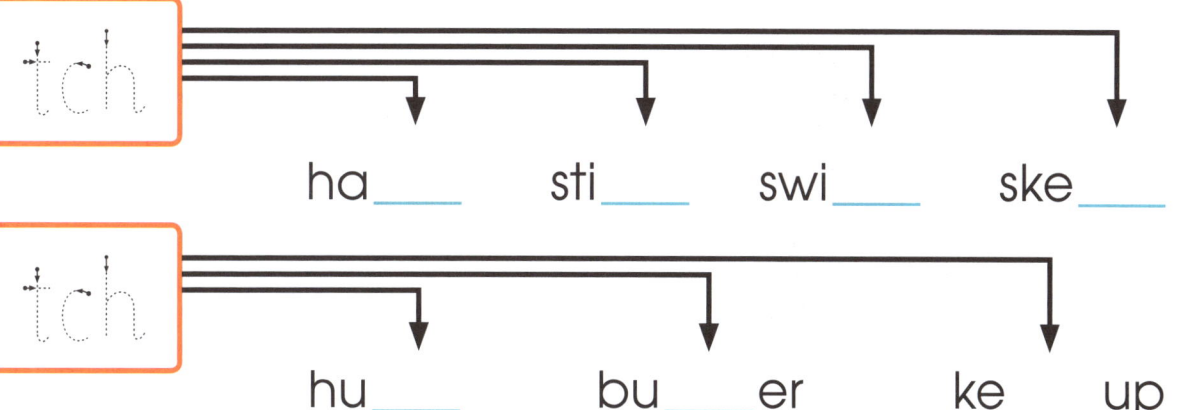

tch → ha____   sti____   swi____   ske____

tch → hu____   bu____er   ke____up

Write the words

Write the words in the grid. Put one sound in each box.

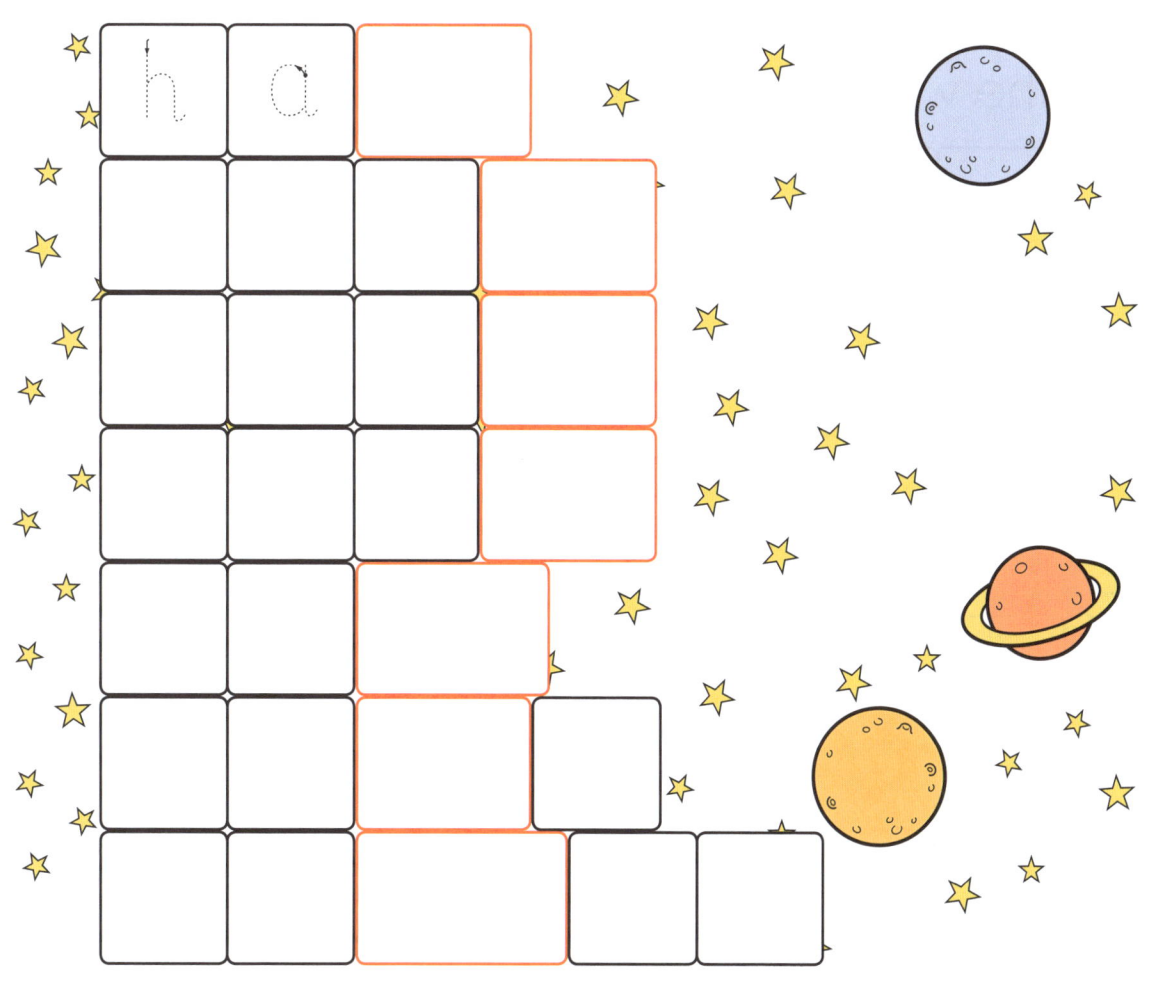

Words with dge

j u dge

judge

b r i dge

bridge

Make the words

Make the words with **dge**.

Read the words. Write the words.

d o   →  _____

h e   →  _____

f u   → _____

b a   → _____

b a   er →  _____

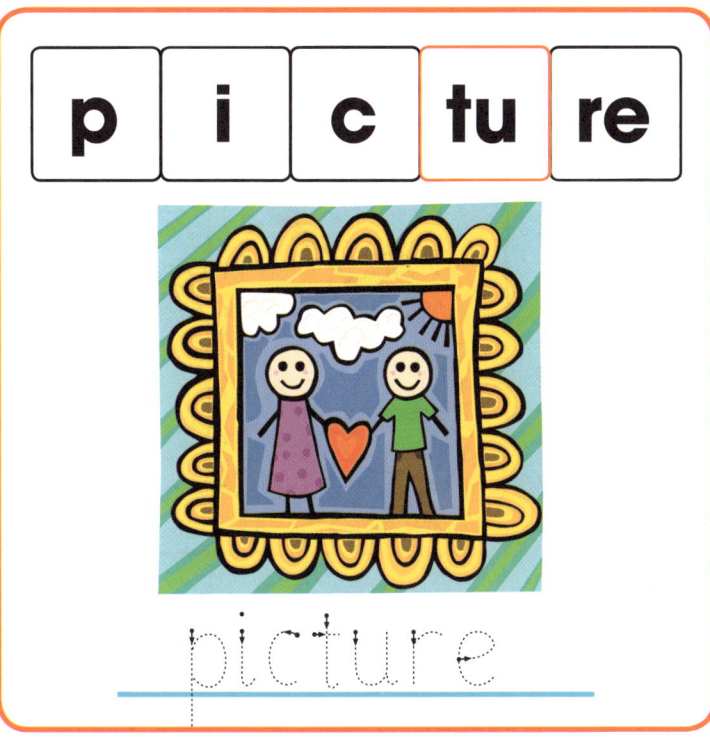

p | i | c | tu | re

picture

Make the words

Make the words with **tu**.

Read the words. Write the words.

n | a | | re → _____

c | a | p | | re → _____

f | u | | re → _____

m | i | x | | re → _____

p | u | n | c | | re → _____

When ch says k

s ch oo l

school

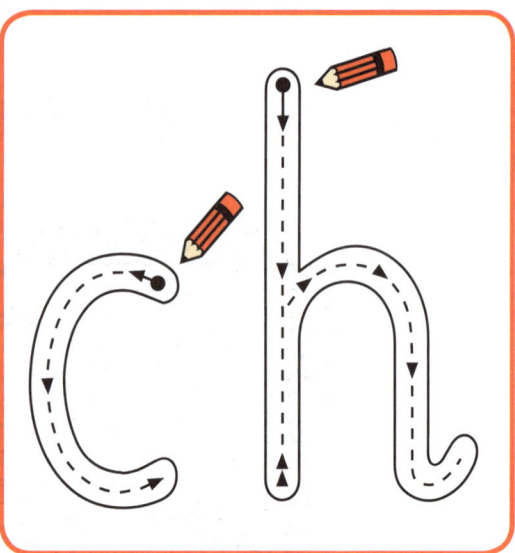

Read the rhyme

Circle **ch** in the rhyme.

One day at home I baked a cake,

But it gave me a stomach ache!

I had to go to the chemist shop

For something to make my stomach ache stop!

When ch says k

Make the words

Complete each word with **ch**.
Read the words.

e____o	s____ool	an____or
____oir	stoma____	____emist

Write the words

Write the correct word under each picture.

_____

_____

_____

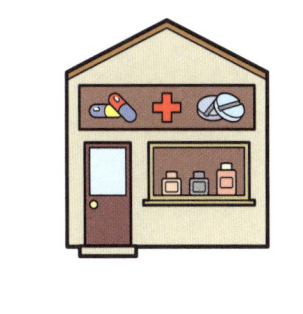

_____

_____

_____

When g says j

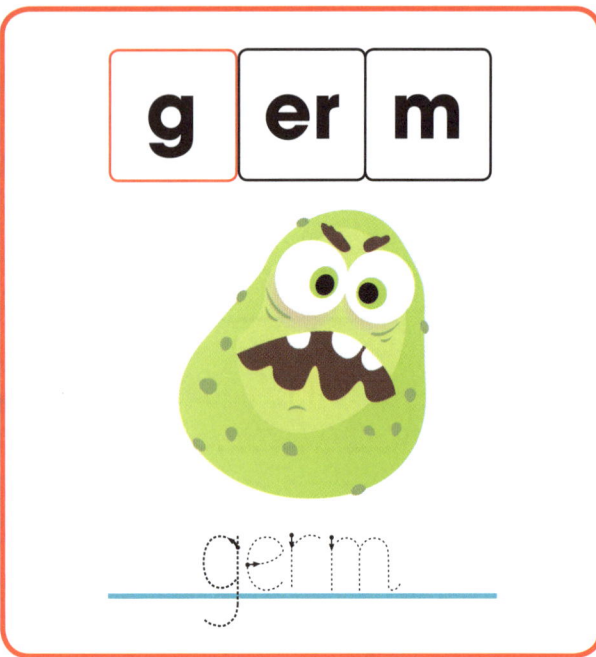

germ

page

Read the rhyme

Circle **g** that says j in the rhyme.

Gina and Gerry live on a barge.

But the barge isn't large.

So it's not at all strange.

That they fancy a change.

Write the words

Write the word for each picture. Read the words.

an_____

g_____

ma_____

dan_____

hin_____

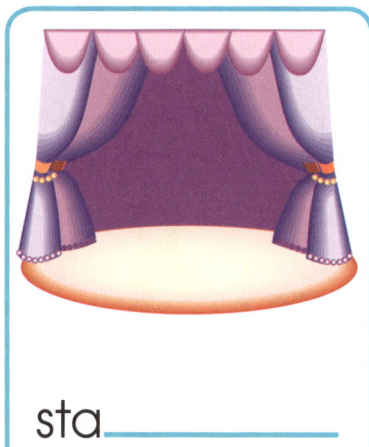

sta_____

Write the words with **g** that says j.
Circle **g** in the words.

A room in a house   loun_____

The front of your hair   frin_____

A boy's name   Ro_____

When s says z

r o s e

rose

h o s e

hose

Read the rhyme

Circle **s** in the rhyme.

The rose grows if I use the hose.

My nose knows when the rose grows!

I suppose the rose knows when I use the hose.

Write the words

Read the clues.
Write the words with **s** that says z.
Read the words.

A food made from milk.   ch_____

Not hard to do.   ea_____

A loud sound.   n_____

A girl's shirt.   blou_____

A polite word.   plea_____

To take your pick.   ch_____

When c says s

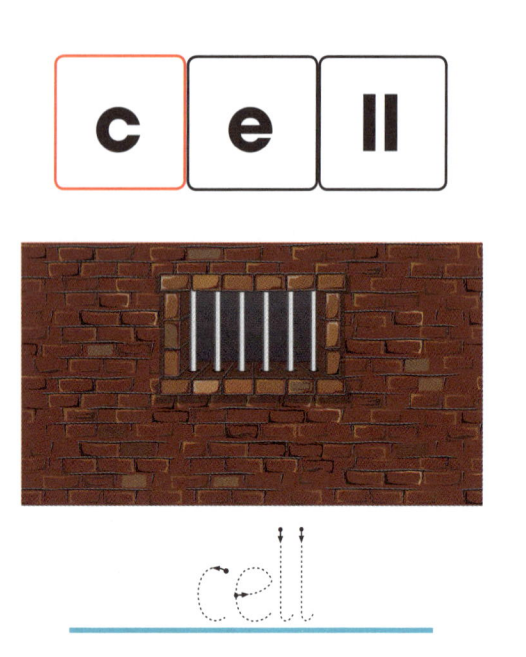

cell

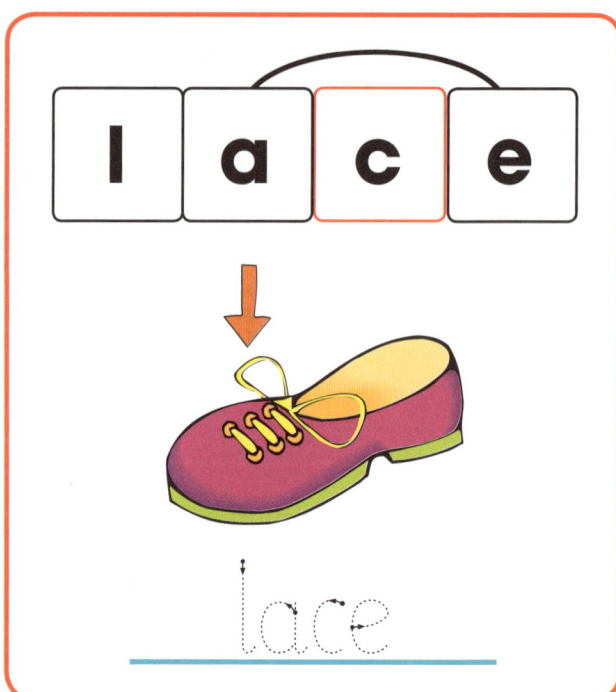

lace

Read the rhyme

Circle **c** that says s in the rhyme.

Cilla went to the cinema
On an icy day in December.
She had no lock for her bicycle
So she tied it to an icicle.

Write the words

Read the clues.
Write the words with **c** that says s.
Read the words.

More than one mouse.   mi_____

This is a smiley   f_____.

A food that goes
with curry.   r_____

White stuff spread on
a cake.   i_____

You roll these to get
a score.   d_____

You run fast in a   r_____.

When ci says sh

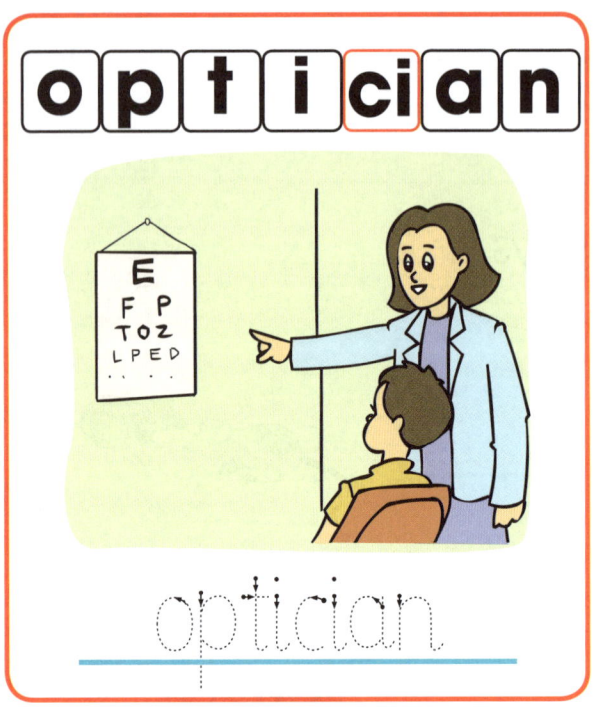

optician

Make the words

Make the words with **ci** that says sh. Write the words. Read the words.

o p t i [ ] a n →

s o [ ] a l →

s p e [ ] a l →

m u s i [ ] a n →

When si and su say zh

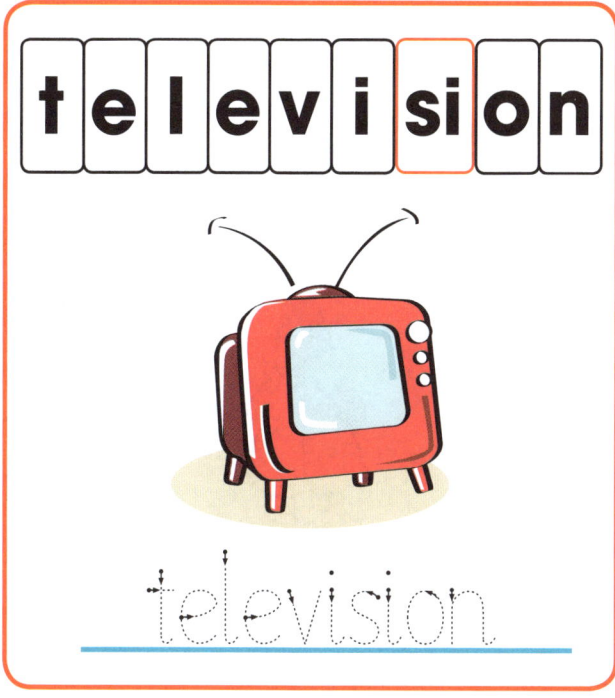

television

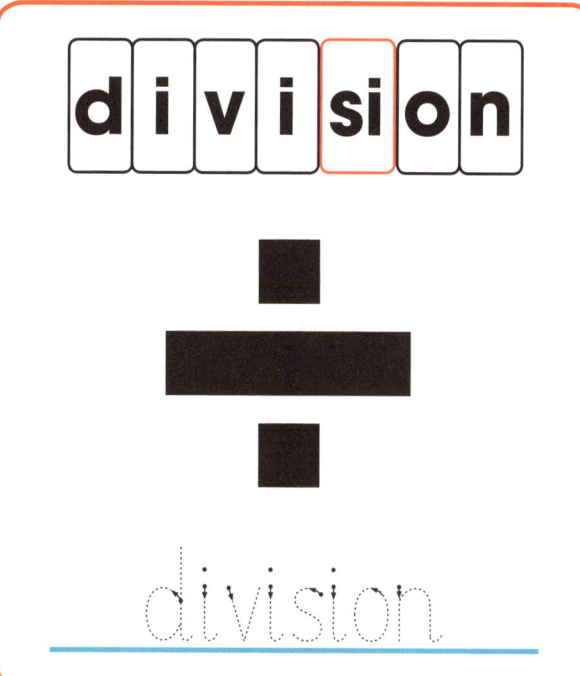

division

Read the rhyme

Circle **s** that says zh in the rhyme.

I look for treasure.
It's a pleasure
To measure the treasure.

When gn says n

sign

gnome

Make the words

Make the words with **gn** that says n.
Read the sentences.

A [ ] **a** **t** is an insect that bites.

A dog will [ ] **aw** a bone.

If it's angry it might [ ] **a** **sh** its teeth.

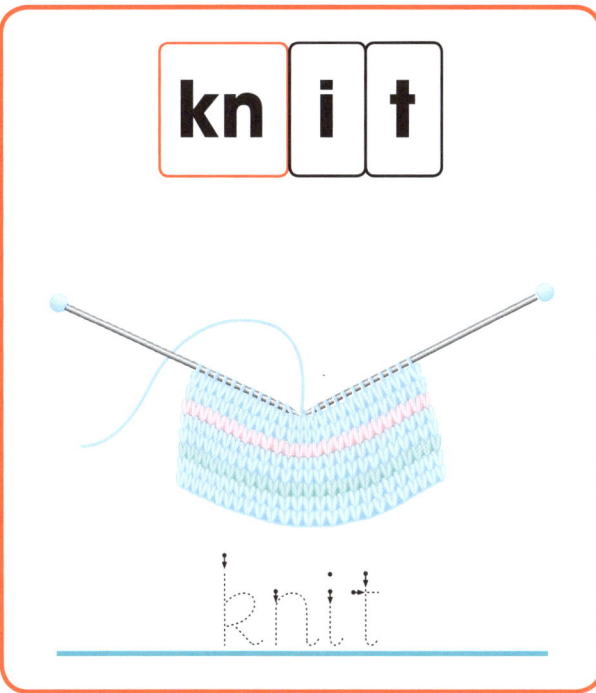

kn **i** **t**

knit

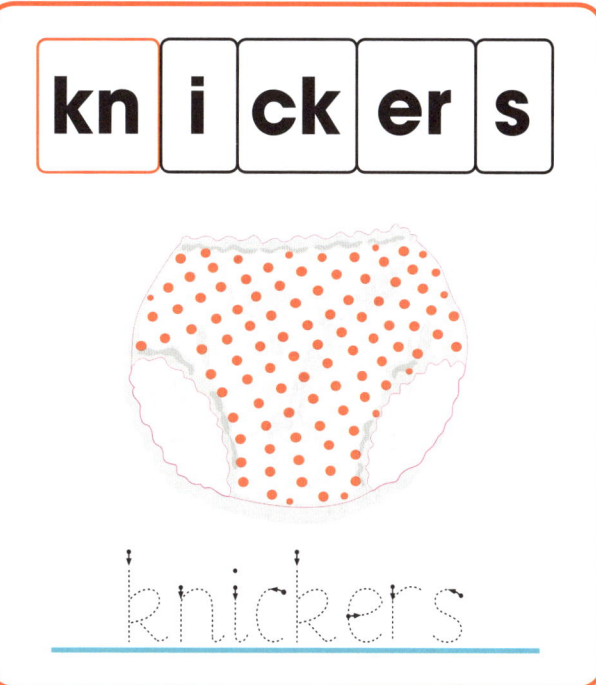

kn **i** **ck** **e** **r** **s**

knickers

Make the words

Make the words with **kn** that says n.
Read the rhyme.

This is the ▢ **igh** **t** that lost his ▢ **i** **f** **e** .

He ▢ **o** **ck** **s** on the door

Where's
my knife?

And ▢ **ee** **l** **s** on the floor.

When wr says r

wren

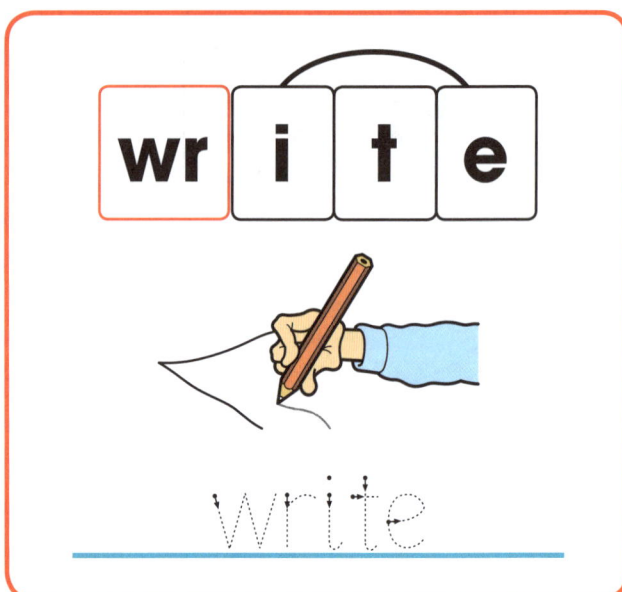

write

Make the words

Make the words with **wr** that says r.
Read the rhyme.

 a word.

It wasn't long.

But the  .

What a **e ck** of a word

I  .

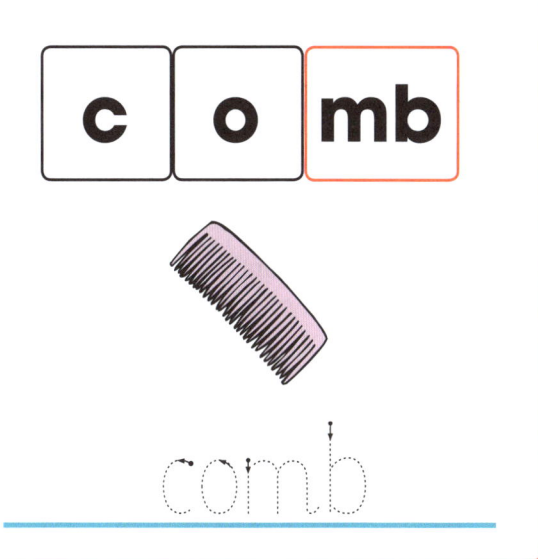

c o mb

comb

b o mb

bomb

Make the words

Make the words with **mb** that says m.
Write the words. Read the words.

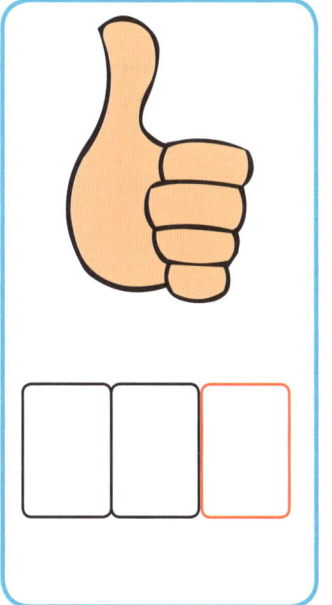

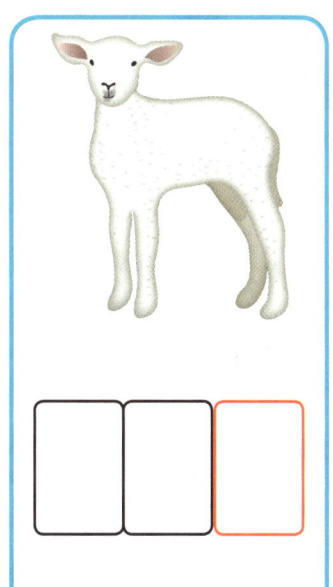

What have I learned?

Note to parents	Present the tests one at a time. Explain that they will show your child what he/she has learned. Use encouraging words such as 'See if you can read the words in this test by yourself'. Tell your child that there will be some words he/she might never have heard before but that they can be sounded using what your child knows about letters and sounds. Explain to your child what to do. For correct answers, use words such as 'Well done', 'You did well.' If incorrect, praise your child for having a try: 'It doesn't matter if you get things wrong. That's how we know what you need to practise.'

Read the words and names.

Test 1

tray	loud
today	Roy
snout	deploy

Test 2

dirt	reach
birch	law
beak	pawn

Test 3

new	Tuesday
drew	Joe
fuel	oboe

Test 4

haul	race
tied	slate
turkey	hike

Read the words and names.

Test 5

poke	tiny
jawbone	limb
tune	acorn

Test 6

monkey	dead
fern	fly
slow	worth

Test 7

calm	spare
heard	cheer
Clare	floor

Test 8

doorway	pour
core	naughty
before	always

Test 9

call	while
install	photo
when	optician

Test 10

match	badge
itch	Phil
fetch	picture

What have I learned?

Read the words and names.

Test 11

kneel	action
chef	badger
obey	echo

Test 12

vision	magic
facial	gnome
gym	adventure

Test 13

wreck	playtime
listen	fairground
fracture	inside

Test 14

sound	borrow
auburn	Stephen
brief	these